D1367593

6-45

GENERAL ADOLF HEUSINGER

SECURITY
AND
REDUCED TENSION

*On the Occasion
of the 70th Birthday of
General (ret.) Adolf Heusinger*

———

4 AUGUST 1967

Published
by Markus-Verlagsgesellschaft m. b. H. Köln
Copyrigth 1967 · Printed in Germany
Translated by Barry Jones
Printers: Greven & Bechtold · Köln

CONTENTS

Professor H. Herzfeld, Dr. phil., Dr. h. c., Berlin

ADOLF HEUSINGER
SOLDIER IN THE "CONTRADICTION" OF HISTORY

7

Brigadier P. Young, London

THE CHIEF OF THE OPERATIONS SECTION

21

General U. de Maizière, Bonn

THE FIRST INSPECTOR-GENERAL
OF THE BUNDESWEHR

35

General L. Norstad, New York

IN THE SERVICE TO THE CAUSE
OF PEACE AND SECURITY

43

* * *

IN THE INTERNATIONAL FIELD

45

General A. Beaufre, Paris

A FRUITFUL EXCHANGE OF VIEWS

51

General (ret.) A. Heusinger, Cologne

SECURITY AND REDUCED TENSION

57

R. Pirk, New York

"ORDERS IN CONTRADICTION"

75

Professor H. Herzfeld, Dr. phil., Dr. h. c.*)

ADOLF HEUSINGER
SOLDIER IN THE "CONTRADICTION" OF HISTORY

Adolf Heusinger's book on the "Fateful Hours of the German Army" from 1923 to 1945 was, as early as 1950, a lasting and valuable documentation of earnest reflection on the convulsion which the standing and tradition of the German army and even the existence of German soldiership as a whole have suffered since the start of World War I. An officer of the Weimar Reichswehr who had served in a strategically important post under Adolf Hitler down to the bitter end on July 20th 1944, has set forth here with unmistakable yet disciplined frankness, his final reckoning on the causes for the German soldier's involvement in the pre-history of

---

* *Professor Hans Herzfeld, Dr. phil., Dr. h. c., who is particularly noted for his work in the field of modern history in the 19th and 20th centuries, was born at Halle an der Saale on June 22nd 1892.*

After attending the Latina of the Francke Foundations in Halle, he studied at the universities of Freiburg and Halle. In 1914 he became a war volunteer and saw active service from 1914 to 1917. From 1917 to 1920 he was in French war captivity. On completing his studies in Halle, he graduated in 1921.

He served first as an unsalaried lecturer at the University of Halle-Wittenberg where, in 1929 he became an assistant professor. After being relieved of his post by the National Socialists in 1938, he was employed as a scientific worker at the War History Research Institute of the Army in Potsdam, but in 1943 he was arrested by the Gestapo. Afterwards he lived as a private citizen in Freiburg im Breisgau.

From 1946 to 1950 Herzfeld was assistant professor at the University of Freiburg, followed by ten years as ordinary professor of modern history at the Free University of Berlin.

Among his publications may be mentioned: " Johannes von Miquel ", 2 volumes, 1938/39; " The Modern World 1789–1945 ", 2 volumes, first in 1952; " The Problem of the German Army 1919–1945 ", 1952; " The Bundeswehr and the Problem of Tradition ", in: Studies of the Political and Social Situations of the Bundeswehr, I (1965), P. 22–95; " The Weimar Republic ", 1966.

the disaster of 1945. At the moment when he was called upon by Konrad Adenauer to cooperate in the re-establishment of armed forces in Germany, a second military career opened for him which led him into the leading supra-national circles of military planning in the Western world – from 1957 to 1961 as Inspector-General of the Bundeswehr, and from 1961 to 1964 as Chairman of the NATO Military Committee in Washington.

In his book, Heusinger as a thinking German soldier of the school of Colonel-General Beck, and as the leading co-worker of Halder and Zeitzler at the head of the German General Staff until 1944, presents his personal summary of events since 1914. In spite of all the additional knowledge resulting from a flood of new literature, this account of the tragedy of "Orders in Contradiction" with its promptly admired graphic objectivity, is an indispensable reflection of the tensions and differences in the mind of the German soldier who has experienced two world wars and two revolutions. Up to now it is one of the most valuable historical testimonies on the catastrophe of the German Army before and during World War II. For the historian in search of a factual appreciation of this development and its conflicts which still stir the emotions today, it is as useful and indispensable now as it was when it was first published.

Without wishing to decide what is to blame in these complexities of a tragically insoluble conflict of duties, the book ends with the statement that here, freedom and providence, destiny and guilt were closely interwoven. The autobiographical motive, however, which pervades its entire contents, is already broached in the first dialogue which Heusinger recounts in his book. This was the conversation between a Reichswehr officer and one of his old war-time comrades in the "Escherich Organization" which took place on the heights of the Thuringian Forest on that fateful night of 8/9 November 1923. What this commanding officer of the Reichswehr battalion declares as his faith when he opposes the threat of force, reveals one of the most profound traits of Adolf Heusinger's, which is confirmed again and again throughout his life: "I am an enemy of all rash action. We – the soldiers after the world war and after the experiences of the Kapp putsch – have every reason to exercise moderation."

The officer of the Reichswehr, the first officer and Chief of the Operations Division in the High Command of the Army in World War II, the man who played a leading part in the build-up of the Bundeswehr, proves himself again and again to be the advocate of moderation and composure. He is imbued with a spirit of responsibility that is always critical even of his own person and with a steadfastness that is deeply rooted in the origins and character of his personality and which has sought to unite the quality of the marked professional soldier with the assertion of man in the human sense.

Born on August 4th 1897 in Holzminden as the son of a respected grammar school teacher, Adolf Ernst Heusinger left the place of his birth together with his father in 1911 and moved to Helmstedt, likewise situated in the Brunswick district. There he lost his mother in 1913 and shortly after the end of the first world war, in 1924, his father also died. His Lower German home and the Humanistic grammar school at Holzminden left lasting marks on Heusinger's character. Indeed, in a speech at Holzminden in 1960 he expressed his sincere acknowledgement and lasting thanks for the knowledge that had been imparted to him there.

On his father's side he came of a bourgeois family of clergymen and philologists dating back to the Reformation. This chain of ancestors was interrupted, however, by one of his great-grandfathers who, as an officer in Napoleonic times, was sent to Ireland whence he brought an Irish wife back home with him. As a forestry commissioner, his grandfather had a profession which, after the end of the first world war, attracted young Heusinger even more than the officer's career upon which he had set out during the war. But in the years of hardship from 1919 until he joined the Reichswehr in 1922 – a decision which was by no means regarded as a mere stop-gap – this profession was not open to him, if only for financial reasons. It is significant that in the greatest crisis of his life, after July 20th 1944 and his subsequent detention until the end of the war, when his life was in constant danger, he sought refuge at Walkenried in the forests of the Harz. Through his grandmother, the wife of the forest commissioner, whose maiden name was La Fontaine, there was also Huguenot blood in this

9

family which, right down to his father, was a profoundly conservative branch of a Brunswick-Lower Saxon family.

The diversity of descent on the father's side, preventing a one-sided restrictiveness, was also effectively strengthened by the influence received from his mother, Charlotte von Alten, who came of one of the most respected noble families in Lower Saxony. In this line, too, there was an officer, General Graf von Alten who commanded the Hanoverian troops at the Battle of Waterloo in 1815. But also the substance of his bourgeois heritage was enriched again from this side, which linked him with the originally noble family of von Campe of Brunswick and especially with the Hamburg publishing family of the same name who renounced their noble rank.

A happy youth whose lasting after-effects have never been entirely lost in the calm and restrained, yet firm harmony of his character, led with the events of World War I to the storms of the 20th century which, from then on, were to accompany Heusinger throughout the whole of his further career. Leaving school at the age of 17 with an emergency school leaving certificate (due to the start of the war), he joined the 96th Thuringian Infantry Regiment in June 1915 as an officer cadet, as a natural matter of course such as was typical of those years. He became a lieutenant in 1916 and was twice seriously wounded: in 1916 at Verdun and in 1917 in Flanders. Following the latter he became a British prisoner-of-war until 1919. This young officer was one of those people who even knew how to make fruitful use of this trying time. He learnt Russian and it may be conjectured that the conscientious composure with which this Reichswehr officer of the Weimar period entered the service of the Weimar democracy was not only connected with the fact that he came of a Brunswick family that originally had stronger ties with the Guelph dynasty than with the Hohenzollerns. Even with his father, there could be no doubt that this family supported the unified Reich of Bismarck. Like many others he was probably also helped by the fact that as a prisoner-of-war, he experienced the catastrophe of the year 1918 from without. In this situation the thinking soldier gained a certain perspective for the passionate differences occurring in the collapse in his native Germany. Things were also made easier for him by the insight he gained into the necessity of the events, through his contacts with the forces on the opposing side.

Since 1922 when he was a young Reichswehr officer in the 15th Infantry Regiment stationed in Kassel, right down to his transfer in the rank of Captain to the Operations Division of the Reichswehr Ministry in 1931, Heusinger had a full share in the work of General Seeckt's hundred thousand man army, the limited future possibilities of which by no means offered a particularly attractive development. It inevitably meant for him the renunciation of politics and the rejection of any new involvement in the internal political struggles – with this position of protection, however, there was also the danger of the "state within the state".

As a generally popular adjutant in the Rifle Battalion in Kassel, he was jokingly referred to by his comrades as "little Ludendorff". In 1927 he graduated from the "Führergehilfenkurs" which was the substitute for the former War Academy, with such success that in 1931 even before the expansion of the army, he was transferred in the rank of Captain to the office of the "Truppenamt" in the Reichswehr Ministry, soon re-established as the General Staff. Under the later Field Marshal von Manstein, he was employed in the Operations Division which became his destiny from 1931 to 1944.

In spite of all his untiring conscientiousness, he was, as a young officer in those years, an evenly balanced character, a great lover of nature and a sportsman, especially a huntsman. His marriage to the art historian Dr. phil. Gerda Krüger who came from Kassel and who bore him two daughters, again confirmed the continued intellectual interests and needs of this soldier; outwardly composed yet not averse to tension-breaking laughter, he is widely esteemed for his human dependability. There is no doubt that this pupil of Beck's and co-worker of Halder's has always belonged to that class of thinking soldier, whose existence in the routine of daily duty would not always have been easy had he not known how to refute the charge so often and easily made of being a "desk theorist".

Owing to the rapid growth of the army after 1933, Heusinger was only able to return to a limited extent, to duty with the troops in the closer sense: 1934/35 in the rank of Captain in Paderborn and especially from 1935 to 1937 as First General Staff Officer (I a) with the 11th Division in Allenstein. Here, to a gruffly conservative

11

Commander who was also terrifyingly frank in his criticism of National Socialism, he was able to supply full proof of his ability to be the heart and soul of a staff. As a militarily recognized "modern" officer alongside superiors of a very much older school, and in a politically tense and precarious atmosphere, he was not only able to play himself fully into the hands of his own staff, but was able by means of gravity and tact and by the ability to exercise relaxing tolerance in the conduct of manoeuvres and map exercises, to have a decisive influence on the training of the troops.

The centre of his work and achievement from then on was the Operations Division of the General Staff to which, on his return from East Prussia in 1937, he belonged without a break until 1944. This was in spite of occasional attempts to return to troop command. He was thus with the General Staff through eight historic years – until 1938 under Beck, until 1942 under Halder and latterly as co-worker of "Kugelblitz" Zeitzler. On the proposal of his predecessor von Manstein, he became Chief of the Operations Division in October 1940, during the tense hiatus between the campaign in France and Hitler's attack on the Soviet Union. He thus became involved in all the conflicts between the military leadership of the army and the interferences of Adolf Hitler. Already under Halder and to an even greater extent under Zeitzler following the Stalingrad crisis and the Caucasus operation, he was a consistent advocate of protest against the National Socialist coercion of the army command by Hitler. At the same time, however, on account of his always preserved composure and as a high-ranking expert, he remained so indispensable, that in the extremely tense months of the early summer of 1944, the period of decisive defeat in Russia and the start of the invasion of Western Europe in Italy and France, that is to say from April to July 20th 1944, he had to bear the full burden of responsibility as Hitler's constant and daily co-worker – the dictator having by then finally broken with the Chief of the General Staff.

A more detailed tribute to the achievements of the soldier Heusinger during these years must be left to a more qualified military pen. Suffice it to say that during the events of the years 1938 and 1939, the "Anschluss" of Austria, the downfall of Czechoslovakia and the preparations for the war against Poland, his criticism was

12

already clearly evident. It can also be stated with certainty today that, as a serving soldier, he must have had a part in the preparation of all operational plans during those years. But he realized from the outset and called attention to the tension existing between Hitler's ultimate objective in this adventure into the vast depth and width (of Russia) on the one hand, and the limitations of the German forces on the other hand, which only permitted the planning of the initial operations. The resistance of the military to the methods of National Socialist occupation policy, which had already been aroused in Poland in 1939, was far more open in Belgium and at first, also in Holland, than in the preparation of the campaign against Russia in which the compliant attitude of the OKW (Supreme Command of the Armed Forces) rapidly led to capitulation to Hitler. This meant that any open resistance on the part of the OKH (Army High Command) to the dictator who was now at the height of his prestige, could no longer materialize.

Following the strategical arguments about the importance of Moscow as an operational target in the late summer of 1941, there could no longer be any doubt about the rejection of Hitler's strategy by the military experts, who had prepared accordingly since Narvik and Dunkirk. Nor could Hitler himself be in any doubt about this since there was, in any case, no longer any question about his basic hostility to all military tradition of the Prussian-German style and above all, to Moltke's well-founded claim for the General Staff to have serious co-responsibility in talks with the man responsible for the policy of the OKH.

For this whole epoch in the life of Adolf Heusinger, therefore, there arises the question as to his relationship towards resistance to National Socialism in the full sense of the word. As a leading figure who lived through and co-acted during that time, he can claim – and this is surely no small achievement – to have faced up to the whole gravity of the problem. And even looking back on the general line of his decisions, there is nothing that he has tried to refute or erase. This is revealed most impressively by "Orders in Contradiction" in that conversation between a soldier (Heusinger himself) and a jurist (his own brother) Dr. Bruno Heusinger, later President of the Federal Court. The conversation took place in the autumn of 1934 and the objective accuracy expressed by

Heusinger is fully confirmed by the brother who, even that time, warned with concern against illusions and had already dared to resist the demand of the personal oath to Hitler. This professional soldier, engrossed in the military work of those years, entertained the illusionary belief at that time that personalities like von Fritsch and Beck would constitute a guarantee for the inner substance of the army, without denying the warning signs of the danger of an inner undermining. But the desire not to allow the army to break up and his motive of revolt against the Peace of Versailles, dominated him too powerfully for him to be willing already at this juncture to give absolute priority to the ethical motive of resistance as the guiding principle of his action following the jurist's warning, over the dream of an inner purge of National Socialism and of a moderation of Hitler as a result of his successes.

Like a *leit-motiv*, this dilemma of conflicting duties is also permeated by all individual conflicts, by a long chain of disappointments in the coming years, which, although not free from fluctuation, is nevertheless by and large of a logical nature. Heusinger who, on account of his calm composure, was undoubtedly better able to get on with Hitler than even Halder and Zeitzler – who were actually the final bearers of military responsibility in the General Staff – and was able, because of this trait in his character, to act as mediator more than once between the OKW – more Jodl than Keitel however – and the OKH and even with Hitler himself. But he also had to make the experience that even the best-meant and best substantiated arguments in favour of a militarily acceptable disposition at the top, broke down hopelessly on the "divide et impera" principle practised by the dictator, whose boundless lust for power hopelessly frustrated any political ending of the war as well as any militarily responsible method for waging it.

Such, too, is the outline of the tragic failure of a military personality who devoted all his energies to the extent of self-isolation and exhaustion, to his duty. A man who was, injured at the side of Adolf Hitler on July 20th, only to be arrested on July 23rd because he was suspected – not without good reason – of having been a member of the plot. There is proof that as regards his mental attitude and bearing and in his innermost feelings, the Chief of the Operations Division was regarded by the most active advocates of military resistance, by men like Stieff, Fellgiebel and above all by von Tresckow, as one of them. This is so, even though they were profoundly disappointed when he tacitly, yet understandably, did not take the final step at their side. Tresckow, as their representative at the Führer's Headquarters, himself tried to become the executor of the assassination plan that was known to Heusinger. It is characteristic that he was promised timely warning to enable him to save himself. But in the precipitation of events on July 20th this did not materialize.

So much is clear, namely that as the soldier ultimately responsible for the wavering Eastern Front and for the coming invasion of East Prussia, two decisive motives restrained him: the hopeless state of the peace probes in the enemy countries and especially in England as a result of the demand for unconditional surrender decided upon at Casablanca. As a result of this, the consequences of an opening of the front in the West whilst resistance continued in the East, became entirely unforeseeable. And then on the other hand there was the terribly oppressing doubt as to whether, after a successful assassination, the army would follow the resistance leadership, or whether it would hopelessly collapse. The situation of the 20th of July is also characterized by the fact that the dilemma of "Orders in Contradiction" had reached its last extreme exacerbation and a personality burdened with decisive responsibility was ultimately compelled to act in accordance with the dictates and within the bounds of his examination of his own conscience.

In connection with the life-and-death months of his imprisonment from July to September 1944, a systematic campaign of calumny has been conducted in East Germany against the Inspector-General of the Bundeswehr. He has been accused of betraying his resistance comrades by the statements he made as a prisoner. The complete nullity and refutation of this propaganda is provided not only by Gestapo material, extremely primitive though its formulation is, reports of Heusinger's interrogation as well as by the memorandum of his imprisonment period found by Percy E. Schramm, by which he by no means became the "father" of the Volkssturm, but which continues the demand made especially in the days around July 20th, that the threat to the German East necessitated the rapid deployment of replacement forces to support the collapsing front. The only people who can object to Heusinger's defence are those who lack any conception of the laws of war and the terror of a revengeful totalitarian force, desperately fighting for its very existence. It is no mere coincidence that one of the men of the 20th of July, General Fellgiebel, himself already lost, defended him in his testimony with heroic steadfastness; and it went without saying that while in custody, Heusinger by undertaking a reversion to his known protest against the top leadership of the army, that is to say against the all-powerful strategic arbitrariness of Hitler himself – a step that was by no means without its dangers – combined his consistent and, from the legal point of view, utterly truthful denial of any participation in the assassination plan. There remains one puzzling element for which there is no rational explanation, namely the fact that the dictator ordered him once more to his Headquarters for a personal discussion – a move that might well have meant life or death. Here, in the course of the discussion of Heusinger's memorandum, Hitler recognized the expert in him, whose services he was reluctant to dispense with, and did so with a slight gesture of personal explanation of that which had been imposed upon him.

Heusinger, however, was neither rehabilitated nor was he assured against further interrogation when he then withdrew to the peace of Walkenried. He had no more protection than other officers in the same situation, against the danger of being on the list of victims who, in the hour of collapse, were to be liquidated at the last moment. It is understandable that a Communist member of his denazification court had very little comprehension of the honourable firmness with which the General refused to allow any obliteration of the borderline that separated him, as an undoubted opponent of National Socialism, from the victims of the 20th of July who were prepared to carry out such extremely radical solutions.

Like other personalities in the German military leadership the General, who was held by the Americans until 1948, was commissioned to submit an expert's report on the course of the war and was also summoned to the Nuremberg Trials as a witness, before he was finally able to retire to private life from 1948 to 1950. These were the years during which he was engaged largely on publishing his account of the fateful years in his book "Orders in

Contradiction". A man who, in his position, had a full knowledge and share in all the military planning of the war until 1944, covering the length and breadth of Europe from North to South, the Mediterranean area, the Middle East and the whole of North Africa, and yet did not lose his inner freedom and the integrity of his conscience – such a man could not simply disappear from history. Consequently in 1950, the year his book was published, Heusinger together with Rommel's former Chief of Staff, General Speidel, was appointed by Adenauer as a military expert to advise on the preparations for the rearmament of a defeated Germany. The former Chancellor chose Heusinger for two reasons: firstly, because in Heusinger he had a soldier of high rank who would be recognized and respected by the Western powers. Secondly, because the ability to apply strictly disciplined service to a difficult task for which Heusinger's career offered the guarantee, now held out the promise of being able to temper the conflicts likely to arise and even of dominating them.

The measure of self-denial that was now demanded of him in this second stage of his military career was to be no less than it was in the crises of the Weimar democracy and in the storms of National Socialism. In the place of sovereignty of the nation that had been gambled away, there now came the link with the allied Western powers, the victor powers of 1945, a link that had become inevitable. The army and the soldier together with German history as a whole had become so problematical, that their revival and restoration were bound to become the subject of prolonged domestic conflict in Germany. In this conflict, the new line dictated largely by the events and the forces of general policy, seemed to some to be too soft judged by the standards of German tradition, and to others too hard and as a reversion to a past that could no longer be defended. The hiatus between the frivolous risk involved in Adolf Hitler's rearmament and the now required limitation of ways and means, demanded a measure of constantly flexible adaptation and subjugation by the soldier to the prime law of politics. This could surely only be effected in responsible quarters by an officer who, in 1950, had really succeeded in learning from the experience gained in a career covering a quarter of a century.

The military answer to the question as to whether Adolf Heusinger has fulfilled this requirement and if so, how, will be given in this book by German and non-German officers, by friends and foes of the two world wars. From 1957 onwards Heusinger, as Inspector-General of the Bundeswehr, held a vital post in these critical years of transition; these were the years during which the inner-German clash of opinion on the question of rearmament as a whole, and also on the inner structure of the new Bundeswehr reached its most passionate heights. They were the years of fierce struggle in connection with the re-introduction of national service, years in which practically all the tradition-bound forces were protesting against the attempt summarized under the formula of Graf Baudissin's "inner leadership", to carry out a thorough modernization of German soldiering, in many cases surpassing the model of foreign countries, as an experiment in the democratization of the armed forces. The task of combining progressive development in this situation with the indispensable use also of conservative forces still linked to the past, was one of the most exacting demands ever imposed on military reformers – reformers, that is, who had only limited political support. It will only be possible to write the individual history of this inner German process as well as the individual history of the incorporation of the Bundeswehr in the supra-national organization of the NATO armies, when a greater period of time has passed. One thing, however, is already perceptible today: Heusinger has continued to stand by the critical conclusions which he drew from the past in 1950. In 1959 he formulated that affirmation of the historical significance of resistance to Hitler that, as a guiding principle, is still valid today. Its lasting content was fully recognized as the indispensable expression of the obligatory power of the conscience – and also as the revolutionary break-through of the strict rules applying to the soldier's duty of obedience. This was done without failing to recognize the possibility of a differently limited decision in the field of defence duty, as he himself had done in 1944. The requirement which he advocates, of mutual tolerance towards differing directions, each filled with the same powerful ethos, is perhaps difficult to bring into line with the call for a radical "overcoming of the past". It is certain, however, that it was the genuine expression of a personality who constantly strove to achieve objective performance in the service of the nation and whose whole life has proved that he was also capable of proceeding from a starting point at the commencement of the century in Germany, along the way towards recognition of its limitations and of the indispensability of its alignment in the further supra-national legalities of an epoch undergoing revolutionary change.

On the whole, then, the picture is of a life devoted to duty and always prepared for change, a life to which the prize of fulfilment of its innermost character can seldom enough be awarded.

Brigadier P. Young *

THE CHIEF
OF THE OPERATIONS SECTION

Chief of the Operations Section General Heusinger was a staff officer, an operational planner, in the tradition of a school that had produced Scharnhorst and Gneisenau, Ludendorff and Hoffmann.

The young German officer who had just left his desk in the General Staff school and had not yet set foot in the grey house on Tirpitz Quay in Berlin felt not only honoured but also somewhat depressed by his appointment to the Operations Section. The General Staff of the Army itself was surrounded by an almost legendary aura, but the Operations Section, its innermost cell, whether in peace or war, had an even more mysterious reputation. And not only in Germany, perhaps even more in other countries the questions were asked: What is going on in the Operations Section? How does it work? To what extent does it influence military affairs?

* *Brigadier (retired) Peter Young, D.S.O., M.C., M.A., F.S.A., F.R. Hist. S., since 1959 Head of the Military History Department at the Royal Military Academy at Sandhurst, was born in London on July 28th 1915.*
After attending the Monmouth School and the Trinity College, Oxford, he was promoted to the rank of second lieutenant in 1939 and served with the Bedford-shire and Hertfordshire Regiment. In World War II he took part in several campaigns and raids: Dunkirk (wounded), 1940; Guernsey, 1940; Lofoten and Vaagso, 1941; Dieppe, 1942; Sicily and Italy, 1943; Normandy, 1944; Arakan, 1944–45.
1953–56 he commanded the 9th Regiment of the Arab Legion.
He is the author of a number of military-historical books: "Bedouin Command", 1956; "Storm from the Sea", 1958; "The Great Civil War" (with late Lieutenant Colonel Alfred H. Burne, D.S.O.), 1959; "Oliver Cromwell and his Times", 1962; "World War 1939–45", 1966. He published numerous articles in Army Historical Research Journal and Chamber's Encyclopaedia. In October 1966 he paid a long study visit to Israel and is now completing a book on the Israeli-Arab War.
Recreations: collecting model soldiers and military pictures, war games.
Brigadier Young married in 1950 Joan Duckworth.

The same questions were asked by a young German general staff officer, a commander of a German army group on the eastern front or – on the other side – by a member of the Stavka in Moscow or, indeed, by a British or American officer working on strategical problems. Even today when new organisational forms of planning and management are being elaborated in research and industry as well as in the military sphere, the study of the Operations Section of the old German General Staff has more than a merely historical or academic interest.

Organisational forms are, however, dead unless they are enlivened and manipulated by men – "what e'er is best administered is best". Therefore, I should like to show the mystical Operations Section at work, through the career of a man who was himself for so many years one of its members and finally, from 1940–44, its chief, and who became in later years (1961–64), at the height of his military career, Chairman of the Military Committee of NATO in Washington – General Heusinger.

The 34-year old Captain Heusinger joined the Operations Section in 1931, at the time of the Weimar Republic. Then, the "General Staff" was not yet in existence – it was forbidden by the Versailles Treaty – but with the approval of the Allies there was a "Truppenamt". Its Section T 1 was charged, as is usual in every army, with studying and elaborating the plans for deploying army units and for their operations. It was a very small section and indeed never grew much bigger. Before the Second World War it consisted, apart from two other officers and some auxiliary personnel, of no more than seven general staff officers. In 1939, when the war against Poland started, there were altogether 17 officers but still only seven general staff officers. And even at the height of the war, from the summer of 1941 until the autumn of 1944, the section had only 14 general staff officers and 13 or 15 other officers.

Heusinger began his work in the Operations Section (1931) in the same way as any other newcomer. It took him some time to become part of this noble circle of "demi-gods" shrouded in the obscure terminology of its Black Art. He was a man of few words and now he became even more taciturn. Learning by listening was highly appreciated and he who "listened in" was, from the first considered to be an equal from whom nothing need be withheld. Heusinger's chief von Manstein, afterwards the famous Field Marshal, soon spotted his talent and later, when he had distinguished himself as the "good star" of the 11th Infantry Division to which he was attached at Allenstein in East Prussia he promoted him (1937) to be First General Staff Officer of the Operations Section.

Heusinger was already showing the qualities which are so valuable in a sphere where the work demands a matter-of-fact approach, mathematical precision and iron discipline. He was accessible to all his colleagues, including newcomers, and radiated calm and prudence. If his views differed from those of his collaborators he put them forward in such a way that they felt he was trying not only to convince but to help them. He never relied only upon his authority and rank. Heusinger was not a "will-power man"; he was sensible and did not demand more from his collaborators than he exacted from himself. He was sparing alike in praise and in reprimand, yet everybody had the feeling that he and his work were appreciated. In short officers liked working with him.

Before we sketch the problems with which Heusinger had to cope in direct confrontation with Hitler, it is necessary to say something of the Operations Section as an institution. Even the non-military reader will appreciate that general staffs date back to the distant days when some farsighted military prince first decided that it was a good thing to have a knowledgeable adviser with him on campaign. Gustav Adolf, King of Sweden, certainly established the preparation and conduct of his military operations according to a well-organized system. France and Prussia further developed the staff system as we know it today. The English system developed rather later and, according to Spenser Wilkinson who had great influence in shaping it towards the end of the last century, derived much benefit from the German model. In 1946, after the experiences of the Second World War, new forms were introduced. The Americans who were the last to develop their system, only doing so after the First World War, took into consideration not only the experiences of others but tried to deal with the ever-increasing need to co-ordinate land, sea and air forces. For the traditional land powers such as Russia or Germany this problem did not yet appear so urgent.

23

The Operations Section took the most prominent place in the German General Staff of the Army. Its chief was the first adviser to the Chief of the General Staff; and his task was the detailed planning, preparation and execution of all operational measures within the scope of the Army. He had to present to the Chief of the General Staff the proposals and suggestions of his section. He also co-ordinated the activities of the Army Command with other headquarters, with other sections within the General Staff and with naval and air forces. The main part of the work involved the drawing up and assembly of large army formations for campaigns as well as their operational control. Though the Chief of the Operations Section had no right to make decisions, this was an advantage rather than a disadvantage since his main task was only to offer his superior various alternatives, a choice between the different operational possibilities. This system worked well as long as the structure of the military hierarchy was maintained, that is as long as senior officers stood between the Chief of the Operations Section and Herr Hitler whose conduct of war the Soviets, not without reason, branded as "adventurist". These men, though some of them had serious faults, had a considerable following in the army and also possessed enough military commonsense to warn Hitler, at least in the military sphere, against the greatest blunder – that of starting a war at all. The Chief of the Operations Section was directly subordinated to the Chief of the General Staff of the Army. Until September 1938 this was General Beck who was one of the leaders of the opposition to Hitler and met his death on July 20th, 1944. His successor, General Halder, retained the post until September 1942 when his serious differences with the Führer came to a head. (He could not, understandably, bring into the open his even more serious moral objections to Hitler; though as early as 1938 he had begun preparations for the overthrow of the dictator.) The next Chief of the General Staff, Zeitzler, was regarded as pro-Hitler but even he was unable to follow Hitler in all his operational decisions, contradicting, as they often did, all commonsense and was deposed on July 20th 1944. Long before that date his frequent encounters with the "world's greatest strategist" had reduced him to a physical and mental wreck. Thereafter the General Staff of the Army was without a chief for Guderian and, in the last months of war, Krebs were only "charged with the management of affairs". Still worse for the functioning of the military machine was the fact that in December 1941, in the middle of the battle for Moscow, Hitler dismissed the Commander in Chief of the Army, General von Brauchitsch and himself assumed command. Already in 1938, after the dismissal of General Blomberg, he had made himself the Supreme Commander of the Wehrmacht. This concentration of functions did not, however, lead to a greater efficiency in the military leadership; on the contrary, it made the operational command of the Army unbearably difficult. Apart from the fact that only the Army was "beheaded" – the Air force and the Navy retained, under Göring and Raeder, their independence and the SS behaved under Himmler more and more like an independent service – Hitler reserved the right to decide even the smallest operational questions and thus practically hamstrung all operations. The mistrusting amateur Hitler was no longer willing to give to the Chief of the General Staff and the higher military commands the operational freedom which is essential for the success of any army.

Another reason for the decay of the German military leadership system was that the Supreme Command of the Wehrmacht held in its hands, in some theatres, operational control over the formations of the Army. This was the case in Norway, Finland, Africa, France, Belgium, the Netherlands and the Balkans. (The Army General Staff retained its original function only on the Eastern Front though this was, of course, the most important.) Thus the High Command of the Army, which was since 1941 in Hitler's hands, and the General Staff of the Army with its Operations Section had parallel organizations in the Supreme Command of the Wehrmacht, whose Staff was under General Jodl. By blindly following Hitler its National Defence Section created endless complications. It could happen that on one front operational command was in the hands of the Supreme Command of the Wehrmacht, supply in the hands of the High Command of the Army, personnel matters under the Army and propaganda under the Wehrmacht.

Despite the fact that the Operations Section of the General Staff of the Army when Heusinger was its chief was in charge of only one theatre of operations, the Eastern, it must be admitted that it was one of the few organizations of the Wehrmacht to remain intact and that it proved a very efficient instrument.

The basic requirement of the Operations Section was a sense of what was relevant and practical. Consistency, and the gift for grasping a situation quickly were regarded as essential.

Heusinger's great advantages were his crystal clear brain, and an astonishing memory and flair for detail. The last was especially important because Hitler liked to hang on to some often irrelevant detail when he wanted to press through his completely different view of the whole problem. Heusinger based his reports on sober analysis and was not afraid to defend them even against Hitler.

The work in the Operations Section was very exacting and the main burden rested on the shoulders of its chief as can be seen from his normal daily programme:

8.00 – Morning report. Account of changes in the enemy estimate. Division of daily tasks among members of the section.

9.30 – Lecture ("Morning Prayers") in the office of the Chief of the General Staff of the Army.

10.15 – Attendance at the lecture of the Chief of the General Staff at the office of the Commander in Chief of the Army (only until 19 December 1941 when Hitler took over command).

11.15 – Reading the mail.

12.30–15.00 (Sometimes longer) – Attendance at the discussion of the general situation in Hitler's office (regularly after 19 December 1941).

16.00 – Consultations with heads of operational groups (each dealt with one army group, and together they formed Group I of the Operations Section).

– Lecture by the head of Group III of the Operations Section which was in charge of organizational problems and transmitted reports to the Supreme Command of the Wehrmacht und its other services.

17.00 – Telephone consultations with the chiefs of army groups on the progress of operations. Consultations with the chiefs of other sections of the General Staff of the Army. Other current matters.

19.30 – Taking the interim reports from the heads of operational groups giving an outline of the daily progress on the front and further intentions of the front commands.

21.00 – Lecture at the office of the Chief of the General Staff.
22.00 – Attendance at the lecture of the Chief of the General Staff at the office of the Commander in Chief of the Army (only until 19 December 1941), then division of tasks among the heads of groups to elaborate the instructions and orders based on the evening lecture.
1.00 and 3.00 – Taking the final daily reports from the army groups. Preparation of the new situation map.

It was important to keep the Operations Section informed as to the situation on the fronts under its guidance, and on other theatres and other services. Apart from the telephone consultations with the chiefs of the army groups there were, of course, other sources of information: liaison officers to especially important battlefields or front commands reported – after the lecture at the headquarters command to which they were assigned – directly to the Operations Section.

Another proven method was to establish efficient sound locators and radio monitoring stations on important sectors of the front; these were in direct contact with the Operations Section. The section also used the services of the reconnaissance air squadrons of the High Command of the Army to get quick information on the situation at the front. Finally, the Operations Section insisted that as many frontline officers as possible came to visit its office from time to time. This was done not only to gain information but also to brief these officers, who naturally knew only their own sectors, on the general situation. Frontline officers who, in 1943, came exhausted and despondent to the Operations Section with such comments as: "You have no idea how things in fact are! Our division does not exist any more!", soon learnt that the Operations Section was well informed even though it had but a limited influence on Hitler's conduct of war.

When such combatant officers came to Hitler's Headquarters to receive high decorations, the Operations Section would try beforehand, in an unobtrusive way, over a drink perhaps, to give them a true picture of the war as a whole which was deteriorating day by day. Characteristically when one of these heroes complained of the "defeatism" of the Operations Section, Heusinger resolutely stood up to Hitler on behalf of his officers who tried to open their eyes.

In what way did the Operations Section participate in the preparation of plans in general?

When in 1937 Heusinger became head of the Group I, with the rank of major, his task was to plan and elaborate all measures necessary for the employment of German forces in case of war. The new "mobilization year" started always on 1 October, but it was impossible in the Germany of 1937, under conditions of constant military-political changes, to elaborate a "deployment plan" as had been usual before 1914 in the Prussian Great General Staff and in the corresponding staffs of other European Powers.

The entry in 1936 of the German Wehrmacht into the Rhineland which had been demilitarized under the Versailles Treaty, the *Anschluss* of Austria in 1938 and the occupation of the border territories and the rest of Czechoslovakia in 1938 and 1939 were not based on plans prepared a long time before. They were improvised by Hitler and indeed the General Staff had warned against them. But the dictator put through his intentions and proved to be right – at least militarily and temporarily. Thus, the General Staff lost prestige – and not only with Hitler.

The *Anschluss* of Austria in 1938 was – referring to the Operations Section – initiated in this way: On 4 March the Chief of the General Staff, General Beck, demanded from the Chief of the Operations Section, Major General Hansen, an outline of the studies which had been prepared several years before for a possible military intervention in Austria. These were in essence of the same character as all theoretical studies in the files of any general staff – incomplete.

The same day the Chief of the General Staff ordered that the study be finished within a few weeks. Five days later, however, it became a matter of hours – the draft of the order for the "possible entry into Austria" was to be ready by 16.00 hours. Hitler was greatly dissatisfied with his general staff: "No, they are not the enthusiasts who made Prussia great! This general staff schooling has its great drawbacks. Prudence, matter-of-factness, caution and thoroughness hamstring courage, resolution and audacity. They see nothing but difficulties everywhere and thrive on worries. All that I have so far achieved was done against the warnings of the General Staff."

These easy victories in dealing with neighbours as France and Britain contributed greatly to Hitler's popularity. General

Halder, who succeeded General Beck in 1938 as Chief of the General Staff, felt compelled to put aside his plans for the overthrow of the dictator. The General Staff, and especially the Operations Section – if they wanted to survive at all as some sort of counterbalance to Hitler and his crew – had to remain intact in their own sphere. And, needless to say, Heusinger, educated as a German soldier, knew his duty – to obey and carry out orders.

Drawing up plans for the Army were based on the Führer's instructions from which the great framework of strategical and operational intentions could be discerned. The operational dispositions of the army groups in large concentrations and the distribution of the formations, the directions and aims of their thrusts were to a great extent Heusinger's work. A former colleague describes his working methods: "It was amazing to watch how in a few hours the picture of the deployment developed on the 1 : 1 000 000 map in the quiet of his locked office. Even after the lecture at the office of the Chief of the Operations Section (Heusinger became its chief only in October 1940) and at the office of the Chief of the General Staff the plan only had to be slightly modified in its basic concept.

It is not possible here to describe in any great detail Heusinger's personal share in producing the various operational plans. However, the planning for the campaign against Russia is of great interest to others beside the military experts.

In the summer of 1940 Hitler came to the conclusion that it would be impossible to invade England and he thought that the elimination of the Soviet Union would be the surest way to break the British resistance later. He was confirmed in his decision by Russia's behaviour in the summer of 1940 and in the spring of 1941 when, after subduing Finland, the USSR annexed the Baltic states, establishing communist rule there. In addition, the Russians were threatening to dominate South-East-Europe, especially Rumania.

The plan of attack on Russia which Hitler made known to the High Commands of the Army, Navy and Air Force in the summer of 1940 was received with serious misgivings. More than once the Chief of the General Staff pointed out the strength of the enemy and the General Staff of the Army delayed the work on the plan. At the end of June and the beginning of July 1940, Jodl, chief of the Operations Staff of the Wehrmacht which was directly under Hitler's command, instructed the General Staff of the Army: It is important to cut off Russia's access to the seas; that means to concentrate the armies on both flanks, in the south and north. Then, on 21 July 1940, Hitler ordered an "assault on the Russian problem" and various authorities began to work on the plan.

The Chief of the General Staff of the Army first made his decision on the basis of the estimates of the Section "Foreign Armies East" and the studies of the Operations Section which was headed from 1 October 1940 by Colonel Heusinger. Also specialists for the eastern campaign, first General Marcks and then the later Field-Marshal Paulus, worked on the drafts. Another operational draft, which dealt, however, only with parts of the problem, was elaborated by several older general staff officers working on a special task ordered by the Chief of the General Staff. The National Defence Section of the Staff of the Wehrmacht was also working on an operational plan.

The plan of the Operations Section of the Army was presented to Hitler on 5 December 1940 and accepted. Yet while its main aim was first of all to destroy the enemy armies, which meant a thrust on Moscow, Hitler came back to his old brain-child of concentrating on the flanks. Despite the representatives of the Army the plan was altered according to his wishes. And to emphasize the "crusading" character of the campaign Hitler substituted the name "Barbarossa" for the original code name, "Fritz".

The "Instruction No. 21 – Case Barbarossa" was sent on 18 December 1940 to the various Headquarters participating in the operation.

The High Command of the Army had now to elaborate the definite drawing up of instructions. Each army group was ordered to try out its task in war games and to test the intended solutions. The army groups, in their turn, instructed the commands of the armies and of the tank groups to acquaint themselves with their tasks, again by means of map exercises. The supply problems were worked out in the same way. And so on down to divisions and lower formations.

On 1 February 1941 the "deployment instruction" was presented to higher authorities but soon had to be altered because of the landing of British troops in Greece and a successful British raid on the Lofoten Islands, Norway (4 March 1941) in which the present writer took part without appreciating its full strategic importance.

At the dawn of 22 June 1941, the German attack on Russia was set in motion.

Several days before the beginning of the war in 1939 the Operations Section had been transferred from Berlin to Zossen, further to the south, and later, in connection with the western campaigns, it had moved to temporary stations in Münstereifel near Cologne and Forges near Namur. From July till November 1940, its seat was Fontainebleau, whence it moved back again to Zossen. In June 1941, shortly before the Russian campaign started, after a short stay in the barracks at Wiener Neustadt, it moved to a large barracks camp in "Mauerwald" near Angerburg in East Prussia not far from the Führer's Headquarters. In this place, aided by the latest transport and communication facilities, the Operations Section remained – apart from a brief visit to Vinitsa in the Ukraine – until the end of 1944. Here, Heusinger, cool analyst and cautious planner, waged his battle not only against the unheard of difficulties at the front, against the vast expanses of Russian territory, dogged bravery of the Russian soldiery and their imaginative leadership, but increasingly against Hitler with his habit of direct interference in the detail of operational planning. Heusinger had to stand up to him in bitter controversy, day after day.

To name only the most serious of these problems there were the great operational decisions taken in the late autumn of 1941 during the battle for Moscow when the Russian armies – helped by the early onset of a hard winter – were for the first time able to seize the initiative (the Zhukov counter-offensive). Then in the winter of 1942/43 the core of the controversy was, of course, Stalingrad where Hitler let a whole army perish rather than suffer a loss of prestige.

It is true that Hitler based his strategical and operational decisions on the need to win the important sources of oil and other raw materials rather than on purely military factors. Yet, he was also moved in his decisions by such considerations as whether the city to be attacked bore the name of some prominent communist

31

leader: Leningrad as the city of the founder of the bolshevik state and Stalingrad as the symbol of his arch-enemy the ruler in the Kremlin.

In his situation lectures at Hitler's, headquarters Heusinger was often advised by Field-Marshal Keitel: "Please, be brief today. The Führer has to be spared. Don't excite him!" To which Heusinger used to reply: "I shall say what must be said."

In his book "Orders in Contradiction" Heusinger reports these dramatic situations in great detail.

Ironically enough it must be conceded that Heusinger had a certain influence on Hitler, of whom he disapproved so cordially. It seems that Hitler himself felt that the prudent approach of the Chief of the Operations Section was better than the rashness of others which led from one catastrophe to another. Even so it usually took a long time before Hitler accepted the proposals of the Operations Chief. Heusinger's situation lectures often took many hours; he returned from them pale and exhausted and used to say to his colleagues in the Operations Section: "I have not had any success today, but perhaps tomorrow..." Then, of course, it was often too late for a successful operation.

Once in September 1942, Heusinger explained to Hitler's Chief Adjutant his attitude to the dictator: "A whole world stands between Hitler and the General Staff. His aversion to intellectual work, his overestimation of all practical activities, his unrealistic exaggerated appreciation of will-power will never allow him to find a true contact with our thinking. Persuade Hitler to give up supreme command, restore freedom of action to the General Staff and the commanders at the front – and you will gain historical merit."

The bomb which exploded on 20th July 1944 in the Führer's Headquarters seriously wounded Heusinger, who was standing next to him giving a situation report, and brought to an end his wartime military career. Together with other suspected officers he was not used any more.

Heusinger's work seems to have totally failed. But the experiences which he had amassed as master of operational planning remained and he was able to use them later for a better purpose in the resurgent army of a new democratic Germany.

It did not fall to General Heusinger's lot to lead great armies in the field, and to British officers, who seldom reach high rank without alternating between staff and command appointments this may seem strange. Yet it has long been the tradition of the German General Staff to develop a breed of coolly analytical intellectual soldiers. Heusinger is the archtype of a school which has influenced generations of military thinkers.

General U. de Maizière *

THE FIRST INSPECTOR-GENERAL
OF THE BUNDESWEHR

We Germans who are said to have a certain tendency to exaggerate in praise as well as in blame, have also become sceptical in our assessment of prominent public figures. It thus happens that we occasionally note with astonishment that a man of our time and of our people is honoured and appreciated abroad almost more than he is by us. I refer to the great sympathy displayed on the death of Konrad Adenauer a few months ago which reminded us of the influence of personality in history.

It is an old thesis: the more the times appear to revolt, the greater is the need for people of firm character, who recognize the possibilities for good, resist all evil and serve as a model for others. It is in this spirit that we soldiers remember on special occasions, those who are outstanding in our ranks. It is a matter of honour and also of gratitude when we look back, on the occasion of the 70th birthdays of the two soldiers whose personalities have left their mark on the build-up of the Bundeswehr: that of General Hans Speidel on October 28th 1967 and today, on August 4th, that

---

* *General Ulrich de Maizière, as Inspector-General since August 1966, the highest ranking soldier in the German Bundeswehr, was born in 1912 at Stade, Lower Saxony. He comes of a family of Huguenots who emigrated from France in the 17th century.*
He joined the Reichswehr in 1930, later received a General Staff training, took part in several campaigns in the East in World War II and served latterly in the Operations Division of the Army General Staff.
On his release from war captivity he became a bookseller and music dealer in Hanover.
Since being appointed to the "Blank Bureau" in 1951, his name has been very closely associated with the incorporation of the Federal Republic in the Western defence community and with the build-up of the Bundeswehr.
General de Maizière is married to the former Miss Eva Werner; they have four children.

of General Adolf Heusinger. I write this contribution with pleasure and at the same time with special respect because, from my long cooperation with these two men, I feel myself as their pupil.

Under the influence of the Korean crisis in 1950, the Federal Government was prompted to give its first considerations to the possibility of Germany's own contribution to the security of Europe. At a remote Cistercian monastery at Himmerod, situated in the valley of one of the tributaries of the Moselle, a group of former officers of the army, the air force and the navy assembled basic material for discussions that were to be held between the Federal Government and the Allies. The meeting had had to receive the approval of the High Commissioners because at that time the Germans could not, in their own right, discuss questions of defence. There was still a long way to go before sovereignty was established. The work of those taking part was determined by the gravity of the situation and the consciousness of their responsibility. Heusinger, an inconspicuous man in mufti, had come from Munich where he had been living since 1948. In his assessment of the situation there was no trace of optimism. But when he then began to discuss new possibilities for the defence of the West, the resignation seemed to disappear. Heusinger once said that fear is a poor adviser. The younger ones were impressed by Heusinger's art of realistically discussing necessities and possibilities and of briefly summarizing them.

It was not long before Chancellor Adenauer also came to appreciate the precision and dispassionateness with which Heusinger formulated and substantiated his military judgements. At the end of December 1950 Heusinger and Dr. Speidel had placed their services as experts at the disposal of the security commissioner Theodor Blank. Adenauer and also the then leader of the Social Democrats, Kurt Schumacher were also among the people who made a profound impression on Heusinger.

The strength of Heusinger's sphere of thought lay, above all, in the field of strategic operations. An officer who, altogether, worked for nine years directly under Heusinger, namely the present Commander-in-Chief Allied Forces Central Europe, General Graf von Kielmansegg, recently said: Even if one were to name all the military leaders of World War II, among whom there were many of great ability, two names are outstanding: Manstein and Heusinger.

And I would like to add: all of us who were able to cooperate with General Heusinger in the preparation of a German defence contribution and later in the build-up of the Bundeswehr, were impressed above all by the way in which he combined the old operative experience with the new circumstances of the atomic age.

The diversity of his ideas was also a help in a question which was widely discussed at that time, namely as to the ratio between military and political authority. Not that he ever questioned the pre-eminence of the political authority. On the contrary. But what would the pre-eminence of the politician be worth in a serious crisis situation, if the military adviser had only one single proposal, only one solution to offer? Heusinger's point of view is this: it is always wrong when soldiers set up a military doctrine and create a military organization accordingly which leaves the responsible politician only a single possibility which is then often no possibility at all. Military thought must be so versatile and the military instrument so flexible that even in periods of extreme tension, the politicians still have alternatives at their disposal.

Anyone who has followed the history of troop deployment plans in the past or the discussion of strategic doctrine of the past few decades will know that such a requirement by no means stands to reason. The offering of alternatives, however, – and this too should not be forgotten – is not only a question of military intelligence but also of personality and of a readiness to restrain one's own person.

Heusinger's call for "modesty" does not mean that in the discussion of purely military problems, the soldier should, from the outset, play second fiddle to the politician. He does not consider it right for soldiers to associate themselves all too hastily with political demands without first formulating with sufficient clarity the military and security-political consequences arising therefrom. But this consideration also means that, in Heusinger's view, the soldier can only give a realistic military assessment if his general knowledge is comprehensive. He mentions as models the great soldierly figures of Scharnhorst, Gneisenau, Boyen, Grolman, Clausewitz.

He recalls that during Goethe's lifetime, almost one third of the people listening to lectures at Berlin University were officers.

This is not the place for a detailed account of General Heusinger's work for the security of the Federal Republic and the free world. Three major periods may be distinguished. First, the years of preparation for the entry of the Federal Republic into the alliances of the free world, 1950–1955, during which Heusinger was latterly head of the military section of the "Blank Bureau"; second, the five years that followed which were of such decisive importance for the build-up of the Bundeswehr, during which Heusinger served first as chairman of the "Leadership Council" in the Federal Defence Ministry and then, from June 1957 onwards, as the first Inspector-General of the Bundeswehr; and third, the period from 1961 to 1964 when he was in Washington as chairman of the NATO Military Committee.

All this can only be portrayed exhaustively within a larger framework. This will be a task for the historians. I will only attempt here by way of a few still topical examples, to record the achievements of General Heusinger for the Bundeswehr during those extremely difficult early years.

It is in accordance with his nature that he kept a cool head in interpreting and assessing the circumstances in which he had to carry out his task. It was therefore not only the existing circumstances but also his own personality that caused him to take considered action step by step. He respected those powers which exercised influence on the new armed forces from the field of politics. His principle was: we must not run our heads against a stone wall!

All those who worked together with him for years on end can confirm the impression which one of his closest co-workers expressed like this: "From the first moment I was impressed with his wise eyes, with which he would look at one almost without the flicker of an eyelid, attentively exploring the mind of his vis-à-vis. He was a master of the art of listening, of remaining silent and of waiting."

This waiting – for which he was occasionally reproached by the less initiated – was not in vain. The public both at home and abroad observed the growth of the Bundeswehr with reservations rather than with favour. During the years of the widespread "without me" attitude to the re-arming of Germany, which the first Federal President, Theodor Heuss, once described as the destruction of all democratic sentiment – many an old soldier would have preferred occasionally to see more energetic action. Heusinger successfully publicized the idea by means of patient persuasion and factual superiority. His restraint did not mean just aimlessly doing nothing. The Bundeswehr grew perhaps more slowly than many non-experts had hoped. But it grew fast enough and steadily into the framework of the alliance. The defence lines of the alliance in Central Europe moved in stages from the Rhine to the borders of the Communist sphere. The purpose of the efforts which the whole nation had to make, was thus fulfilled.

Another example is provided by the "inner leadership". The task of adapting human leadership and soldierly order to the requirements of modern arms technology and to the conditions of our present day society, could not have been carried out had not Generals Heusinger and Speidel been convinced of the rightness of these aims and had they not assumed the military responsibility for the solutions that had been arrived at. The human side – as Heusinger once put it – must be brought into unison with military necessity. Even after the first World War many of these thoughts had already been in the minds of young officers, but these efforts had then been killed. "The incursion of politics into the sphere of the soldier with the abundance of tasks and problems of modern war, makes our limited conception of the ideal training and education for the officer such as Seeckt had in mind, in need of revision."

Heusinger was never the man who merely told people what they wanted to hear. Certainly, he was sincere. The story in a magazine of how, during manoeuvres, the highest ranking officer in the Bundeswehr "addresses a very young lieutenant with a slight frown" and then, "in order perhaps to soften the somewhat awe-inspiring impression of his strict general's face (and the shining general's stars), smiles reassuringly after his first sentence" – this description is probably true. He said to everyone what was necessary. But he said it from a warm heart. He restrained the "reformers" from taking any excessive steps. To former soldiers

he not only reaffirmed that we in the Bundeswehr must be profoundly convinced of the need for the further cultivation of the
supertemporal, ethical values of soldiering, he even went so far
as to tell them: "Tradition is not the petrifaction of all that which
has now become partly more or less coincidental. When in the
first decade of this century the introduction of field-grey uniforms
was debated in the Reichstag, there were some who opposed this
necessary demand of the hour, on the grounds of tradition." In
the times of the Reichswehr serious consideration was given to the
retention of the lance. When the Bundeswehr was created, some
people became rather agitated at the idea of NCO's going out
without bayonets. And so Heusinger kept an open mind towards
all new ideas. But he could become very cool if new regulations
were not decided upon from the point of view of objectivity.

At an early stage Heusinger devoted his career to tasks connected
with higher leadership where he so proved himself that especially
during the war years, his work in these high offices of leadership
could not be dispensed with. However, his responsibility as the
highest ranking soldier in the Bundeswehr did not allow him to
forget that all action of leadership concerns the men in the com-
pany, the squadron and the group. To high-ranking leaders and
General Staff officers he repeatedly urged the need to remember
the rank and file: "Without a deep inner understanding of all their
worries and needs, of all their feelings and thoughts, no one will
be able to subsist. Listen to the call of your hearts, Gentlemen,
even when, in difficult decisions, you have to silence it."

Heusinger's way of looking at things and of expressing himself
is not the easy-going, equivocal way as is testified by his order of
the day on the occasion of the 15th anniversary of July 20th 1944
when he placed the happenings of that day in their right light. For
a time, that day seemed to the German soldier to be an event that
could only be faced up to with difficulty. Heusinger paid tribute
to the action and the sacrifice of those men who had risen up
against injustice and bondage out of a burning anguish of conscience and had tried to eliminate the "Supreme Commander"
who had himself renounced all ethical obligations. But he also
paid tribute to the soldiers of World War II who, from the point

of view of their sphere of responsibility, had believed that they should fight loyally on. For him the moral attitude on which the action of the individual is based, is the connective link and thus the solution to the tension which is only seemingly insurmountable.

In the factual field the Bundeswehr owes its training in the cooperation of the partial armed forces up to the level of a united Bundeswehr way of thinking, to its first Inspector-General. Heusinger pointed out the serious faults in German military organization during World War II when army, air force and navy carried out their operations to a large extent independently of one another. In his conception, the strategic importance of the elements land, sea and air must be constantly revised and coordinated in connection with the ever-changing political, economic and arms technological developments. Soldiers who are repeatedly confronted with the difficulties of their arms systems, extremely great though they may be, are sometimes in danger of capitulating, in the actual practice of training, to the primary demand for the specialist. For this very reason, the higher up we are, the less we should allow ourselves to be diverted from taking the general all-round view.

The history of the Bundeswehr includes the mastering of the technical, tactical and strategical problems of nuclear arms and the answering of the questions which conscience poses with regard to the use of such weapons. Heusinger once said: "In view of the possibility of nuclear war in which earthly goods like house and home, wife and children may be destroyed, it is not easy to answer the question as to the appositeness of the soldier's fighting. If man regards the preservation of his own biological life as the ultimate point of his existence, and if he is unable to sacrifice its temporalness for higher ideals – then it is practically impossible to induce in him the right attitude towards living and dying." The formula which Heusinger found was, that especially after the experience of bitter abuse in the past decades, the soldier's moral code must be oriented to man. The ethos of the soldier's service is to be there for "others", to protect them to the extent of his own renunciation and sacrifice, faithful to his vow and to his oath on the flag. He endeavoured to convince us that the Bundeswehr should be and is nothing more than the visible expression of our defence will, a part of those forces which our people need if they are to live in peace and freedom. As a believing Christian he unerringly advocates the view which the great English soldier Marlborough once put into these words: "No vocation needs religion more than that of the soldier. We must take the people under our care."

When General Heusinger retired from active service on February 29th 1964 he had – to quote his own words – in the 49 years of his military career "had to savour all the heights and depths of our profession and yet never lost faith in our profession". Since then he has not been idle. He continues attentively to follow developments, as was revealed by his lecture at Heidelberg University in the spring of this year on the subject of "Security and Relaxed Tension" the text of which has been included in this booklet. Even today he continues to lend an ear to the problems of the Bundeswehr – an army which, like all armed forces in all countries, is never really complete. But when he speaks to one of us today, then it is always with the reminder that the longer one has been out of active service, the more risky it is to give advice, because one is then no longer fully informed. And so he informs himself always very thoroughly before he speaks – that too, is his way.

The Bundeswehr can give no better present to its first Inspector-General on the occasion of his 70th birthday than by remembering his postulation: "If everyone in his place does his duty conscientiously, we shall fulfil the mission we have been set."

General L. Norstad *

IN THE SERVICE TO THE CAUSE
OF PEACE AND SECURITY

Dear General Heusinger,

On the occasion of your anniversary, I should like to convey my warm congratulations. The great family of nations allied in the cause of peace will not forget your distinguished name. The German soldier stands high among the armed forces of the Alliance and has earned a fine reputation as a dedicated representative of a democratic country and as a faithful servant of the Alliance. In great part this achievement reflects your own qualities and results from the example you have set. We are all greatly indebted to you for your service to the cause of peace and security.

I should like to return to you today the farewell words which you addressed to me in Washington in 1963 when I retired from military service: Our best wishes accompany you and at the same time the hope that you will always stay in contact with us.

* *General Lauris Norstad, New York, was Supreme Allied Commander Europe in the decisive years when the German Bundeswehr was undergoing its initial build-up.*

43

* * *

IN THE INTERNATIONAL FIELD

When in January 1951 Lieutenant-General (retd.) Adolf Heu-singer and Lieutenant-General (retd.) Dr. Hans Speidel were appointed as military advisers to Chancellor Adenauer's Defence Commissioner, Theodor Blank (member of the Bundestag), hardly anyone can have realized that, for these two officers, this would mean the beginning of a second military career so to speak. On the Petersberg on the other side of the Rhine from Bonn, a conference started in that month of the three High Commissioners of the United States, Great Britain and France who were responsible for the democratization and also for the security of the new German Federal Republic. It was from this beginning that the Bundeswehr and the German contribution to the defence of the Western world subsequently emerged.

Heusinger had already worked together with the Western Powers when, soon after the war, he helped the Historical Division of the US Army to throw a little more light on the true story of the German Wehrmacht under Hitler.

But the Americans should also learn that he was far from becoming a mere US "fellow traveller". In 1956 when Admiral Radford, then Chairman of the Joint Chiefs of Staff, had proposed a drastic reduction of the US Armed Forces, because conventional forces might be replaced by nuclear weapons and when rumors were even spread that America might revert to an isolationist position, Chancellor Adenauer was alarmed and sent General Heusinger to Washington to find out how matters stood. At that time the Bundeswehr which, in personnel strength, is today the largest army in Western Europe, had scarcely ten thousand men. If the U.S. divisions were to be withdrawn from Europe, wouldn't that just be inviting the Soviets who at that time were very active, to invade Western Europe? And if all defense were to be based on the "big stick", or "massive retaliation" would the American people really be prepared to reply with the nuclear strike, thereby risking enemy strikes at the American continent with atomic weapons if, for example the East German People's Army which in those days already numbered a hundred thousand men, were to occupy German towns like Hamburg or Brunswick close to the Iron Curtain? Heusinger, then Chief of the Military Council in the brand-new German Ministry of Defense, was given an assurance that the "Radford Plan" was not exactly what the newspapers had written about it and that it did not constitute US policy. No reduction of American forces stationed in Europe would take place "for the time being". And beyond this Heusinger not only learnt that Admiral Radford is an honourable man with whom he could converse well, he not only found in General Taylor, then Chief of Staff of the Army, a kindred spirit, but he realised too that American problems as world problems could be very complex and pressing.

As, after the failure of the plan for a European defence community, German re-armament was only to be put into practice within the framework of the NATO, it was only natural that the highest ranking soldiers of the Bundeswehr should come into particularly close association with SHAPE, the Allied High Command in Europe. During the period under consideration here, the supreme commanders were General Gruenther, followed by General Norstad and finally General Lemnitzer.

General Lauris Norstad held this important post from November 1956 to January 1963. This meant that he had contacts with General Heusinger both before Heusinger became Inspector-General of the Bundeswehr in 1957 and later, in 1961, when he was elected Chairman of the highest NATO military body, the Military Committee in Washington. Altogether this association between the two men continued for seven long years so that for this reason alone, it is appropriate to report at somewhat greater length on the cooperation between Norstad and Heusinger. It should be stated, however, that the relationship between General Gruenther and Heusinger was by no means of an inferior nature – Gruenther was especially impressed by Heusinger's great strategic talent. General Lemnitzer made Heusinger's acqaintance when he was still Chairman of the United Chiefs of Staff in Washington and when, on account of his official position as top-ranking soldier of the US forces, he adopted what was, perhaps, a more national American standpoint than an Atlantic one. But when Lemnitzer was himself appointed Supreme Allied Commander Europe, he already knew that he would then acquire an even better understanding with the "Atlantic thinking" Heusinger than before.

It is said that in character, Heusinger and Norstad had something in common. Maybe Norstad's "northern heritage" – his ancestors came from Scandinavia – and a good portion of Irish blood in Heusinger's veins had their effects. In his family there were many clergymen and Norstad's father, too, was a minister of the church. The fact that, after a hard military upbringing, both were engaged at an early stage and for a long period on such humdrum work in the field of planning and operations, also played its part. But it is certain that both preferred to approach problems with thoroughness rather than in a light-hearted way.

The problem was: on the one side, the Soviet side, there were at that time 175 front divisions to which 300 further divisions could be added within three weeks – and these figures do not even include the Soviet satellites; on the western side, on the other hand, there were only 30 NATO divisions. Although by July 1st 1957, that is to say shortly after they had been enabled to participate in the defense of the free world, the Germans had already established three divisions and placed them under NATO command, it was Norstad's duty to press for the rapid creation also of the other German divisions – 12 in all. General Heusinger explained the difficulties to him: there was a shortage of barracks and of material. There were also considerable psychological difficulties in a country that had previously been subjected to thorough de-militarisation. But the Federal Republic was, after all, the first country in the alliance that advocated the intregration of logistics. The Federal Republic was the first to advocate the build-up of its armed forces as part of an Allied force instead of as national forces.

There were hundreds of problems, the difficulties of which lay in the psychological and the political rather than in the military sphere. Reference is made here to the example of the establishment of the Baltic Command: for five years there were negotiations within the framework of the NATO with Denmark and the Federal Republic of Germany until an acceptable solution, both politically and militarily, was found. The question was whether Denmark which was of considerable importance in the defence line of the alliance, should come under the command of Fontainebleau or Oslo, in other words where was the borderline to be drawn. Should Danish troop units be placed under the command of a German after the bitter experiences of the second world war were still vividly remembered in Denmark? Could the Germans, who were numerically stronger, be expected to submit permanently to a Dane? Ultimately a mixed staff was formed, the leadership of which was entrusted first to a German and then to a Danish commander. This solution, like many others, was the result of infinite patience. As regards German-Danish relations, it is, perhaps, significant that the Danish ambassador in Bonn at that time, Mr. F. Hvass, still has friendly memories of General Heusinger as "a fair-minded man of good and upright bearing". It should also be noted that M. François Poncet – to mention another man – who, in 1951, was Chairman of the three High Commissioners and French ambassador in Bonn and one of the best experts on Germany – before World War II and afterwards – today still has friendly links with General Heusinger and who said of him the other day: "I have always esteemed him as a man of sound common sense and acumen, very balanced in his judgement, very human, very considerate and open-minded to objections and contradictions, reliable and loyal in his relations with others. He always appeared to me to be a decided partisan of the Atlantic Alliance and of close cooperation with the USA and with the other NATO powers, a man with a warm-hearted devotion to the European idea and to Franco-German rapprochement."

When General Heusinger was summoned to Washington in April 1961 as Chairman of the Military Committee in Permanent Session, he did not yet realise that he would regard his work in this highest NATO military body as the crowning of his military life. He once confessed the misgivings he felt at first: "I was deeply concerned about several problems: for the first time in my life I had to live for some years in a foreign country – and this at my advanced age of 64. Would I be able to adjust myself to this entirely new environment? As a German I was to enter the highest military authority of the alliance of nations against which Germany fought during two world wars. How would I be accepted? For the first time I had to work at headquarters, the decisions of which have to be unanimous. Could this work be successful?"

This work was successful for otherwise, his term of office would not have been prolonged on expiry of the originally prescribed period of two years. And although he did not act like a "Prussian" – American journalists said he was more like the "American officer type" – he evolved decisive concepts for the improvement of the work: "Our Western military alliance differs from that of the East in that it is not just commanded from one point, but its problems are brought to solution in joint work. But this system can only be successful if the military-political questions are dealt with by one body – the North Atlantic Council as the supreme organ of the NATO which is composed of the representatives of sovereign states, by the Secretaries of Defense and of State – and if the major, purely military questions are likewise handled by one body – the Military Committee in Permanent Session and by the Standing Group."

Heusinger who was not one to thrust himself to the fore, knew how to win over his partners – even in Washington. Mention may be made, for example, of the representative of France on the Standing Committee – General A. Beaufre and his successor, Admiral M. Douguet, or the representative of the United States in that same body, General Clark L. Ruffner. And then there was also Admiral Lord Louis Mountbatten of Burma who, like the Chiefs of Staff of the armed forces of the other nations, frequently had dealings with the Military Committee.

Heusinger always strove for "a lucid concept for the Chairman". On this he conducted many talks and consultations. It was at this time that the idea of a true "forward" defense and the plans for a mobile task force were realised in the NATO. The assessment of the situation led to the proposal for the build-up of a medium-range ballistic missile force in Western Europe in order to give us parity with the Soviet forces. The ideas revolved more and more around the problems of atomatic armament. Actually it was always a question of "flexible response".

Heusinger's work in Washington, however, went far beyond the Military Committee and the Pentagon where his office was located in the same building as that of the Chairman of the Joint Chiefs of Staff. In numerous lectures he sought to create understanding of the importance of questions of international security. Thus he not only addressed the US Army War College or the Naval College but also the Center for International Affairs of Harvard University, for example, or the Graduate School of Business Administration, University of Virginia.

When Heusinger left Washington in February 1964 and afterwards retired altogether from active military service, the senior officer on the Military Committee, the Portuguese General P. Rodrigues, told his colleagues there in the course of a speech: "By his integrity and his devotion to the ethos of the soldier's profession, General Heusinger brought high repute to the post he held which, until then, had enjoyed but little authority. In our office he successfully brought about a discussion of the problems and a really free exchange of views on them which greatly contributed to the success of our work. We have all greatly esteemed his wise and statesmanlike advice. Although it is difficult to break away from national ties, he was entirely impartial in the conduct of his supra-national post."

This impartial form of conduct should be the supreme duty of all those who wish to serve the cause of real peace in the international field.

General A. Beaufre *

A FRUITFUL EXCHANGE OF VIEWS

My first meeting with General Heusinger took place in 1952 in Bad Neuenahr where, as a Brigadier-General, I was in charge of a tactical study group that had been created by the Supreme Allied Commander Europe (SHAPE) in order to examine in what manner modern tactical ideas would influence the war of the future. The aim was to draft an interallied tactical regulation.

At the time it had been said to me: "As the Germans will come some day in any case, it would be useful to familiarize them officially with these studies now, so that later we do not have to start all over again." In Paris General Hans Speidel referred me to Heusinger. At that time they were both still wearing civilian clothes – the one as military adviser in the alliance preparations, and the other working at the Bureau Blank in Bonn. That was the start of close cooperation and of a very fruitful exchange of views.

* *Army General André Beaufre who is regarded as one of the most stimulating strategic thinkers in the Western world, was born on January 25th 1902 at Neuilly-sur-Seine.*

After attending the military academy at Saint-Cyr, studying political science and passing out of the General Staff Academy, he served in Algeria and Morocco, was in the Soviet Union in 1939 and, from 1940 onwards, belonged to the French High Command. From the outset he was in the ranks of the Free French in North Africa; later he took part inter alia in the campaigns in Tunisia, Italy, France and Germany.

After World War II he held, among other posts, that of assistant to the Commander-in-Chief in South-East Asia, Marshal de Lattre de Tassigny, in 1956 Army Commander-in-Chief of the French Expeditionary Corps in Egypt., 1957 Deputy Commander-in-Chief of the French Forces in Germany, after which he became Assistant Chief of Staff of Supreme Allied Commander Europe and in 1960 French representative on the Standing Group in Washington.

Since his retirement in 1961 he has become widely known through his numerous books, such as "The Art of Total War in Peace", "Deterrent and Strategy". He is Director of the French Institute for Strategic Studies.

In 1948 he married Geneviève Douvry; they have two children.

In Bad Neuenahr I discussed with General Heusinger the results we had arrived at in our studies. When he came to me with some of his colleagues, I asked him for his advice and I very soon gained the impression that we were going to get on well together. In this respect there were no difficulties between German and French military men; our armies had clashed so often in the past that we Frenchmen reached more rapid agreement with the Germans on purely military matters, than, for example, with the British. The lessons the Germans had learnt from the war were noticeably the same as the ones we had learnt. At that time we did not hold any grand philosophical discussions on strategy, but simply spoke about the problems under discussion, about attack and defence, about delaying tactics in battle etc.

Heusinger agreed unreservedly with the conclusions we had drafted in Bad Neuenahr with regard to tactical procedure and the forces. We realized what the defence requirements were in those days, even though our studies within the framework of the alliance, were not put into practice.

Our ways crossed again several times. I followed Heusinger's rise to the top of the Bundeswehr with great interest. I knew to what great extent he had played his part in the build-up and the mental re-orientation of the German armed forces. I also knew his book on the German military resistance and appreciated his attitude all the more since we in France have also experienced the conflict of conscience by "Orders in Contradiction".

Nine years after Bad Neuenahr we were to work together again in Washington in 1961. I represented my country there on the Standing Group, a three-power committee consisting of one American, one British and one French representative. Its sessions were attended by the Chairman of the Military Committee, the highest military organ of the NATO, as a kind of "sleeping partner". This Chairman of the Military Committee in Permanent Session was General Heusinger who, up to that time, had been Inspector-General of the Bundeswehr. Thus I was able to follow from close quarters the fresh impulses which he brought to this inter-allied body which was already threatened with stagnation by routine. On Heusinger's initiative and suggestion, a kind of integrated planning staff was created within the framework of the Military Committee in

Permanent Session from which the International Military Staff as it exists today evolved. Heusinger no doubt desired to review the necessity for the existence of the Standing Group which constituted the executive organ of the Military Committee in which not all members of the alliance were represented but only the "Big Three". (Since July 1st 1966 when France withdrew from the organization, the Standing Group has ceased to exist.) In order to clarify somewhat the position Heusinger held in Washington, it should be borne in mind that the Military Council supplies military advice to the North Atlantic Council, that is to say to the highest political organ in the alliance, and lays down guiding principles, recommendations or instructions for the subordinate supreme commands and offices. At that time this was still done via the Standing Group.

Like Heusinger, I was convinced that the military disposition of the alliance still contained weaknesses and above all, that our defence planning for Europe cannot be regarded in isolation from the great problems of world strategy. We were very well aware that we lacked the real overall view which alone permits essential decisions in strategy to be made. We strove to establish this all-round view. In numerous discussions of the major questions of the alliance, I found that our views largely coincided.

General Heusinger stayed on in Washington after I had taken my leave and had evolved my conceptions of strategy in a number of books which I know my German colleague read with interest. After all, I had gained the impression that, like myself, he was convinced of the necessity to align the strategical decisions inside the greater political framework and that he was imperceptibly moving away from the purely operative way of thinking with which he had grown up, towards a more "global" perspective of strategy. The fact remained, however, that in contrast to my own way of thinking, he still clung basically to what I should like to call the "Atlantic conception". For him, agreement with the powerful American ally was the fundamental prerequisite for the protection of Europe. To this imperative he subjugated the greater independence of the continent in matters of defence which I hoped for and which I regarded as essential especially after the events of the Cuba crisis. He und I both regarded Franco-German cooperation as the necessary supplementation of a common defence alliance.

I know that Heusinger has developed from the concept of

purely military strategy in the direction of total strategy. This is evident from his writings and his pronouncements, as it is from his assessment of the strategic world situation in 1954, 1960 and 1962. I always had the impression, however, that the experiences of the last war, the campaign in Russia and the Battle of Berlin had a very lasting effect on his thinking and that he was always concerned in the first place with defence, the military repulsion of an attack, and not so much with how the deterrent manoeuvre could be brought effectively into play in peace time. Seen from the German point of view, this is no doubt understandable. For the Germans Russia is near whereas we in France are one row farther away from the Russians, so to speak, where it is easier to philosophize than when one is in the front row.

As regards the assessment of the given tactical and military situation, I fully agreed in my analyses with Heusinger. On one point which, however, is no longer a matter for the military but for those who bear the political responsibility, our views probably differed. I refer to the famous controversy as to whether one should plan in accordance with the enemy's intentions or in accordance with his actual and existing military potential. The answer to this question must quite obviously determine the entire orientation of defence policy; it is, moreover, of decisive importance for the conduct of deterrent strategy in times of peace.

Within the bounds of the classical military view, the possible "intentions of an enemy" are left out of consideration. But the very expression "intentions of an enemy" implies that we really are concerned with an „enemy", whereas in peace time the fact whether anyone is an enemy or not, is determined by his intentions. In my view this is today one of the major problems. The fact whether the Soviet Union is an enemy or a "non-enemy" changes everything. It is much more important to know this than to know the answer to the question whether the Soviet Union is in a position to do this or that. American military power, for example, does not worry France, because the United States are not our enemy. If we were to become the enemy of the United States, everything would be different. To put it in other words: I believe that today when we are formulating a strategy for peace time, it is necessary to introduce this important factor here, namely the question of "intentions" even though it is very difficult to handle. If one were to confine oneself to the problems of potentials, then France would have to adapt herself for defence against Spain, Italy, Germany, Great Britain, the United States etc. And in view of the political intentions displayed by these countries, this would be utterly senseless.

In this question, therefore, that is to say the question as to whether the intentions or the potential of the other are more important – and this means ultimately, more important for the concept of total strategy, General Heusinger and the majority of his colleagues still seemed to cling more to a purely military way of thinking which, no doubt has its justified origins, but which does not necessarily always comply with present-day developments. With the Germans more so than with the French and especially more than with me, the operative attitude predominates, fostered and upheld by the proximity of the Soviet army and by the idea that Germany might again become a battlefield. In 1953 in Bad Neuenahr we were already confronted in our studies by the problem of having to bear in mind the possibility of nuclear bombardment during the fighting on German territory and to assess the possible consequences of such a kind of warfare.

Today I am convinced that such considerations which were no doubt contemplated in many armies, are a thing of the past and that we are now faced with entirely new problems. But I am also sure that particularly General Heusinger is one of those who have recognized these new trends and who are endeavouring to draw the proper conclusions arising from them for the defence of Europe.

The high esteem of my German colleague's military qualities and the respect for his personality are based, therefore, on the conviction that here is a man who has outgrown the purely military framework and who has recognized the great political dimensions in which decision on war and peace is taken today against the background of mutual deterrence.

General (ret.) Adolf Heusinger

SECURITY AND REDUCED TENSION*

Security questions and reduced tension are today in the forefront of all political activity. They are the problems of world politics as well as of the NATO. They are the expression of the conviction that only by their solution can the world be given the peaceful consolidation for which it is striving.

Twenty years of development since the last war have been unable to eliminate the great antagonisms in the world between rich and poor, between the starving nations and those living in abundance, between the white and the coloured races, between Communist and non-Communist states, nor have they been able to abolish thoughts of power on this earth. Rather have these twenty years of development exacerbated the situation through the rise of Red China and of many newly-created, economically weak states. In many cases they are incapable of democratic forms of government and – in their struggle for industrial modernization – can often only be ruled by military dictatorship which, in the long run, is an unhealthy system; they are states which, although they would like to play an independent role in world affairs, are incapable of doing so.

For twenty years the UN has been trying to overcome the world's trouble spots, unfortunately with only limited success. Its efforts are often thwarted by voting procedures and it possesses no powers of authority with which to assert itself. However, one should not lose hope, for it has indeed become difficult, in view of the political machinery of this world organisation, to unleash a major war.

In these twenty years, moreover, the realization has gained ground that a great war cannot solve the world's problems but would only result in chaos. The conquest of time and space,

---

* *Lecture delivered at Heidelberg University on January 11th 1967.*

the production of weapons of mass destruction and the sweeping progress in technical developments make any great military clash appear absurd. The world has become small and outer space has drawn nearer to us. And so today, it is hoped, we are at the beginning of a new era in which a solution to the world's problems will be sought in a reduction of tension and thereby in international cooperation and not in military confrontation. The deciding factors in such a development will continue to be the two giant powers – the United States of America and the Soviet Union. Whether war is prevented and real peace established will depend on their conduct. Today no other power can match them, not even Red China. And so to begin with, I should like to draw a comparison between these two great powers.

They face each other on the inner and on the outer line. The East, on the inner line, feels itself encircled by the United States and their allies and is striving to break out of this encirclement and to procure new space in the world for Communism. The West, on the outer line, is endeavouring to prevent any expansion of the Communist sphere of power.

In spite of these opposing and fundamental objectives, it is possible to detect a number of views that are common to both. On the one hand there is the clear intention to avoid a major war under all circumstances. On the other hand there are the common endeavours to seek reduced tension and disarmament. Thirdly, both are striving to preserve the existing alliance systems and thus to guarantee security. There still remains, however, the profound ideological gulf between Communist thought and the freedom-loving, democratic outlook of the Western world.

The difficulties facing the East in the achievement of its objectives lie firstly in the relations between the Soviet Union and Communist China whereby it is evident that Red China is making genuine and realistic territorial claims on the Soviet Union. Furthermore there is the liberalization that is going on in Russia herself with its consequences in the economic and ideological fields. And then there are the diffractive trends in the satellite countries together with the economic difficulties that are constantly arising in the Eastern bloc. In addition it is possible to detect a weakening of the revolutionary impetus of Communism as a whole.

58

The West is also confronted with similar difficulties. There are firstly the differences of opinion in the NATO on many world problems. I need only mention Vietnam, East-West relations, the assessment of the enemy situation, the racial question – I am thinking of Angola and Rhodesia –, the part played by the United States in the alliance and the position of France. These differences of opinion have led to signs of a loosening in the structure of the alliance such as have occurred during the last few years as a result of France's efforts to detach herself from the close bond of the alliance. There are also the financial problems. There are a number of states in the NATO that are not in a position to meet their financial obligations. And finally the NATO has lost much of its original impetus in the same way as Communism has. It has always been strong whenever there was a threat from the East; it always became weak when Khrushchev and the other Soviet leaders smiled.

In this way a crisis has developed in NATO during the last few years. It may be stated, however, that this crisis has not led to a dissolution of the NATO but that NATO is on the point of mastering it.

A military comparison of the two giant powers leads to the following result: on the one side there is a strong land power – with an unbroken land mass, with superior conventional forces and superior medium range missiles – and on the other side there is a group of sea powers with superior naval forces, with superior intercontinental potential but which are dependent on sea links.

Some figures may serve to clarify this comparison of military power. In the field of existing nuclear potential, the West possesses a fourfold superiority over the East. But even the East has a potential of such strength that they are in a position to inflict severe blows on the West and particularly on America. From this, there arises what is known as the nuclear "pat".

In the sector of strategic nuclear weapon systems there is likewise an approximately fourfold superiority in intercontinental bombers and intercontinental missiles on the Western side, a twofold superiority in nuclear-powered submarines and about 22 aircraft carriers on the Western side, compared with none on the Eastern side.

In the case of tactical nuclear weapon systems, on the other hand, there is clear superiority on the part of the East. They possess considerably more continental bombers and about seven times as many continental medium range missiles.

As for land forces, the East has about a hundred divisions ready for action compared with about 28 of the West. In the case of the tactical air forces of the two sides, there is approximate equality whilst the West has a clear superiority in naval forces with the exception of the conventional type of submarines. Of these, the Soviets have about twice as many as the West.

By and large the comparison of military forces leads to the following picture: Western superiority in the field of strategic nuclear weapon systems and in naval forces is confronted by a clear superiority of the East in conventional land forces, tactical nuclear weapon systems, and in conventional type submarines. And there is approximate equality in nuclear potential – if one looks at it in the way I have stated – and in the field of tactical bomber aircraft.

In this military comparison, it may be some consolation to note that within two thousand years of history, whenever a great land force and a great naval power clashed in the course of hostilities, it was always the naval power that gained superiority and decided the outcome of the war in its favour. In the modern age of nuclear weapons, it is true, this may only apply under certain conditions.

During the past ten years the rate of economic growth in the East has been unmistakable. But in spite of this, it has not succeeded in decisively overtaking the economic capacity of the West. Thus, in steel and mineral oil output, that of the West is double that of the East and the superiority in electric power production is even threefold. If the West continues to maintain its present output level, the East will not succeed in acquiring economic parity with the West, especially in view of the fact that as a result of the liberalization trends in the East, its demand for consumer goods has increased, which means that the available funds for military armaments can no longer be employed one hundred per cent as used to be the case.

If we look at the comparative forces of the two great powers in this way, the question arises as to what importance Western Europe can have at all within the framework of this world situation. Let me answer this question by putting forward the problem: what would happen if Western Europe were to be lost to the East?

It would mean that not only 300 to 350 million people would fall into the hands of the East but also 30 per cent of the world's mineral oil production, 30 per cent of the steel output, 25 per cent of the coal and 25 per cent of the world's electric power. This would give the East an obvious superiority over the West. In addition, the loss of Western Europe would probably also involve the surrender of Africa to the East. The world would be divided into an Asian-European-African bloc on the one side and an American on the other. The superiority of the former, especially in the economic sector, over America would amount to as much as 50 per cent.

A principal source of danger to Western Europe is the inner undermining of the defence will of the European nations in consequence of the very skilfully pursued policy of co-existence on the part of the East. The consequences of this inner undermining might be very serious and might, in the course of the years, lead to the East recognizing a possibility for successful subversive activity.

The military threat to Western Europe lies in the Near East, that is to say in the southern flank of the NATO. If the East were to gain possession of this territory, it would not only gain free access to the African continent by land. It would also break open the southern flank of the NATO and seriously threaten the Mediterranean area and possibly even gain possession of it.

The second danger zone in the military sense is Scandinavia. If the East were to succeed in gaining ground here and in bringing this area into its sphere of influence, the northern flank of the NATO would be broken open.

The principal danger spot continues to be the central European region, that is to say the area between the Alps and the North Sea. If the Soviets were to thrust forward to and across the Rhine, the European defence would be penetrated in the centre and defence of the continent would no longer be possible. This danger in the centre of Europe is particularly intensified by the medium range missiles which the Soviets have stationed on the Polish-Soviet frontier and which constitute a mortal threat to the whole of Europe.

In this situation, the fateful factor for the Federal Republic is that its territory is decisive for the defence of Western Europe and thereby for the defence of the whole of the Western world.

The defence of Western Europe in the central region, however, suffers from a number of serious weaknesses. For instance, the defence front has no operative depth. In the age of modern arms development, a few hundred kilometres no longer represent the operative depth of former times. Secondly, the defence of Western Europe has no natural obstacles. Even the Rhine in these days of modern engineering equipment, is no longer a natural military obstacle. Thirdly, Europe is entirely dependent in its defence on the United States and alone cannot guarantee its defence. Western Europe is today, perhaps, already a third power in the economic sense; in the military sense it will not be able to develop into an independent third power. It must further be borne in mind that the reserves that could be made available for the defence of Western Europe are located far away, on the other side of the ocean in the United States and would first have to be moved up in long-term operations. Europe alone would be surrendered to the clutches of the East were it not for the support in the rear of the United States.

A comparison of military forces in Europe presents the following picture: the following forces are available in the central European region: on the Eastern side about 40 divisions, on the Western 24; on the Eastern side the 40 divisions have 30 further divisions ready for action behind them, whilst the West has seven. There is, therefore, an obvious superiority on the part of the East. If we express this in figures for some of the branches of weapons, we find that in the case of tanks there are 20,000 on the Eastern side and 5,000 on the Western; the East has 6,000 cannon compared with 4,000 of the West; and there are 1,400 rocket launchers in the East and none in the West. The East thus possesses overwhelming superiority in conventional weapons.

In spite of this, however, I doubt whether, in the Eastern view, a superiority of 40 divisions over 24 divisions would be sufficient for the staging of a surprise attack. In the Soviet view threefold superiority at least, is needed for such an attack. And so one can speak of a certain balance of power in the field of conventional arms in this central European area, assuming that only those forces that are directly available are taken into consideration.

As regards the air forces the East has a superior number of bomber aircraft whilst in naval forces they have a clear and, in part, overwhelming superiority in the Baltic Sea: three times as many destroyers, three times as many motor torpedo boats and seven times as many submarines.

Of decisive importance for the military situation in central Europe, however, are the 700 medium range missiles that are ready for action in the East and which constitute a mortal threat to Europe. In addition the East has the advantage of initiative, for it can be assumed that the West will never itself be the aggressor. The East thus has the possibility of combining its forces in individual areas in a powerful focal point. And finally, its reserves are nearer and more accessible than those of the West. The longer a war lasted, therefore, the more the power ratio would change in favour of the East.

In this assessment of the situation, it is necessary to avoid any possible wishful thinking. We are not so much concerned with finding out what the Soviets want in the military and political sense *today*. Our assessment must be based on what they *could do* if they wanted to. In view of this situation of Western Europe which, in spite of all the recent loosening tendencies, must continue to be regarded as extremely grave and which, at any time, is liable to become critical again, the question as to how this danger can be countered, must be examined.

In my opinion the security of Western Europe should be sought in three ways and all three must be pursued simultaneously and uniformly and should not be adopted separately. They represent at the same time the strategic concept of the NATO and are basically recognized by all its members as binding. There is no agreement, however, as to the methods whereby these three courses can be successfully adopted.

The first way is by means of an effective and plausible deterrent with the object of preventing war from breaking out at all. By this deterrent it shall be made clear to the potential enemy that he cannot achieve his political ends by military means; indeed, in this way, he would run the risk of committing suicide.

The second way is by the maintenance and presence of such powerful military forces in Europe that for each member of NATO, defence from its own frontiers, that is to say the so-called "forward strategy", is guaranteed. Without this guarantee the very heart of the alliance would be endangered. Countries situated close to the frontier, like Turkey, Greece and the Federal Republic of Germany would feel they had been deserted and would lose their interest in the alliance.

The third way is by attempting to reduce tension and by relaxing the present hardened situation, in order in this way, to initiate a fundamental change in the political situation and to seek security in that very political development. For us it is of particular value because only in this way could our reunification, in all probability, be brought about.

Let me examine these three possibilities more closely:

The first way, namely the deterrent was, for years, guaranteed by the clear nuclear superiority of the United States. But since the state of nuclear "pat" has come about, this kind of deterrent alone is no longer plausible. The Soviets are well aware that the Americans, in view of the danger to themselves, only regard the use of their nuclear potential as the ultima ratio, when all other military media have failed. A deterrent that is based solely on the threat of the great nuclear strike – described as the massive reprisal – also ties the hands of the politician in his freedom of action, if it is proposed as the only possibility of military defence. It must be the task of the soldier, especially in times of tension, to leave the politician – as far as he justifiably can – the scope for political measures and not commit him merely to a military possibility. The West, moreover, might find itself in an extremely difficult moral situation if, for example, the Soviets, in view of their conventional superiority, were to solemnly declare prior to the start of hostilities, that they would renounce the use of nuclear weapons so long as the West did likewise. This is a perfectly conceivable possibility. This would shift the entire moral responsibility for nuclear war on to the West if it had prepared no other means of defence; and this would be an almost unbearable responsibility.

The deterrent must, therefore, be of as varied a design as possible. A flexible method should be aimed at. The potential enemy must be kept in the dark as to how the West will react to his aggression, whether it is conducted with conventional or with tactical nuclear weapons or even by the great nuclear strike. This very uncertainty as to the Western reaction will make the risk involved in an attack all the greater and will exhort him to exercise caution. This flexible form of deterrence calls for balanced conventional and nuclear forces and takes into account a possibly very varied war scene.

This war scene is more uncertain than ever. Even before 1806, from 1914 and 1939 onwards, the experts were entirely mistaken in their prognoses as to a coming war and how it would be fought. How much more difficult it is today, in view of the unsolved problems of nuclear war, to form an accurate idea of such a war.

Let me put a few questions to which no one today can give any positive answer. If war should come, shall we have to expect a long or a short war? Will it be a nuclear or a non-nuclear war? Will the use of nuclear field weapons and nuclear tactical weapons necessarily lead to the use of the great nuclear potential? And finally, a very important and still unsolved problem: Who will have the greater advantage from 'he use of nuclear weapons, the aggressor or the defender? All these problems are unsolved. It is, therefore, necessary, to issue a grave warning against any expectation of a decision being brought about only by the use of one particular weapons system. This has always been wrong. I regard conventional hostilities as more likely than nuclear and I feel that preparation for them is particularly important in our situation. True, – and this must be noted here – there must be no hesitation in the timely use of nuclear operations if there is no other way of halting aggression. We Germans have no desire to be conquered again.

The views held in the NATO as regards the question of a plausible and effective deterrent differ. Whereas France and Great Britain would like to give priority, in spite of everything, to the massive threat of a reprisal strike, the others favour the flexible theory. For years past a settlement or compromise has been sought here. Indeed this is practically the main problem facing the NATO. I believe, however, that we have reason to hope that a solution will be found.

Economic stability in the West must also be regarded as a factor of deterrence and thus also of security. If it were to be lost, the readiness of the Western nations for defence would decline. The East could exploit such an opportunity by means of subversive measures, or even by military action.

Deterrence includes above all, however, – and this is often overlooked in present-day wishful thinking – the firm political will of the NATO nations to defend themselves if necessary with all available means. It seems to me that today, as a result of the loosening and break-up symptoms arising from the co-existence policy of the East, this clear attitude is threatened. Vigilance is urgently needed. Policy can rapidly change but the inner attitude of a nation cannot be changed so quickly.

Deterrence and with it, security, are thus resting on three pillars: the military, the political-economic and the internal political-psychological. If one of these pillars were to collapse, the entire deterrent would be called in question, and this would bring the danger of war closer.

However, should the deterrent fail, no matter for what reason, the question as to how "forward defence" is to be ensured, would move up into the foreground; this is the second NATO problem and it is particularly vital for us. With 24 divisions and a front line of 800 kilometres from Passau to Lübeck, one cannot be equally strong everywhere. The weak forces when deployed linearly, would be split up and overstrained. There would be the danger of a break-through which could not be halted. It will therefore be necessary in the decisive sectors – between Lübeck and the Elbe and between the Harz Mountains and the Main – to hold the front tenaciously on the ground, whilst on other sectors operating a mobile defence and throwing back the temporary invader by the employment of suitable reserves, and restoring the line. The forces available at present might suffice for this so long as they only have to deal with the enemy forces in Czechoslovakia, Poland and East Germany amounting to about 35 to 40 divisions. If stronger enemy forces are to be expected immediately from behind the front, they will not suffice. The question of a nuclear strike will then arise at a very early stage. Any reduction in the Western conventional forces that is made without similar action on the other side, therefore endangers not only the deterrent effect but also the forward defence.

Even the idea of balancing a reduction (in the conventional forces) by a "big lift" from the United States, i. e. by bringing up reserves from the United States by air in time for effective use on the front is, at least at present, a pious wish. Such a "big lift" would have to take place in times of tension. If it is only undertaken after hostilities have started, it will be too late – if only on account of the landing facilities in Europe. However, whether the politicians, in times of intense political tension, will give the green light in time for the start of such a large operation and thus deliberately risk a further exacerbation of the situation, is questionable to say the least. Whether the formations would reach the front in time, is uncertain. The danger of Germany, in particular, being overrun, would be very great. I will not exclude the possibility, however, that with a change in the all-round political situation and with further technical developments, such an amendment in the conception of defence and with it, also in forward defence, may, at some later date, be conceivable. At any rate, today any unilateral reduction in troop strength without any equivalent action on the other side, is a dangerous undertaking.

Alongside these basic factors of deterrence and forward defence for the security of Western Europe there have now been for some years past, the efforts to bring about a relaxation of tension and to guarantee security in this way. The trends towards relaxed tension occur on three levels – the political, the military and the nuclear level. As part of developments in general, they rest in the desire to transform the confrontation of the two giant powers into cooperation in the interests of peace, to limit the arms race in the world and to bring about a mutual reduction in the financial sacrifices devoted to military purposes. These endeavours are only to be welcomed, especially as it is only in this way that the re-unification of our country can be achieved. We should, however, assess the possibilities dispassionately and realistically and should not jeopardize our security.

On the political level these efforts to bring about a reduction in tension started more than ten years ago.

In the plan of the Polish foreign minister Rapacki, the different variations of a neutralization, a de-nuclearization and even a complete de-militarization of Germany and also of Scandinavia were suggested. In this plan, the position of Poland and Czechoslo-vakia remain obscure as also does the question as to what extent the Warsaw Pact and also the NATO are to be preserved. Rapacki is probably primarily concerned to manoeuvre the Americans out of Europe and in this respect, his ideas have the approval of Moscow. But a certain interest in the Scandinavian countries and Great Britain cannot be denied. For us, some of the ideas are worthy of consideration; on the whole, however, the plan endangers our security if it threatens to isolate us. Only a broad neutralized belt from Scandinavia to the Balkans which would include Czecho-slovakia, Poland, Hungary and Bulgaria could be considered.

In the course of time further ideas of a European security pact evolved from this plan. But they involve the risk of separating Europe from America. If this risk were to be avoided, however, they might well constitute a serious plan for the future.

De Gaulle's visions may also be regarded as an attempt to bring about a reduction in political tension. His ideas foresee a new Europe extending as far as the Urals, as he once said, at any rate including Russia, thus entailing the dissolution of the two present power blocs. This new Europe, according to de Gaulle, should develop into a third power, be independent of America and again assume a role such as Europe has had for centuries. The question-able aspect of this plan, apart from the separation of Europe from the United States, would appear to be the re-awakening of old national states and thus the danger of new rivalries in the future between the individual nations. It might constitute an evil reversion to a dangerous past. Moreover it should not be overlooked that in such a Europe, Russian preponderance would be inevitable and American support in the rear might be lacking. The Soviet attitude to this plan is one of 'wait and see' since it also provides for the dissolution of the Warsaw Pact.

At the same time there has been an increasing development of ideas in the United States on the subject of reducing tension which the Americans are so urgently striving for. A considerable part is played in these ideas by internal political factors and by a certain discord over the all too small contributions by Europe in the field of defence. Other contributory factors are the difficult situation in Vietnam and the dispute between Communist China and Soviet Russia. These ideas are based, on the one hand, on the belief that America and Europe must remain indissolubly allied together and, on the other hand, on the desire for an urgent easing of the tension in Europe and it is realized that an objective start must be made from the present status quo. On the other hand, how dispassionately responsible Americans like McNamara appraise the actual situation is shown by what he said in his annual report to the United States Congress: "Western Europe remains the most important group of states to which the United States is closely and necessarily allied. Everyone, including the Soviets, is fully aware that an attempt by any hostile power to dominate or gain control over Western Europe's 350 million people, its immense material resources, its strategic positions, would directly affect the vital interests of the United States. It is equally clear that the close link and the alliance with the United States provide the other member states of the NATO with the best possibility of protecting themselves. At present Vietnam is the acute problem facing the United States, but it should immediately take second place to Europe if the free world were to be challenged in that continent."

These efforts to reduce tension in the purely political field are being accompanied more and more by the economic trends in both East and West towards closer cooperation. Finally, there is also the keen endeavour of the Federal Republic to establish closer contacts with the East bloc countries.

In all these ways a gratifying effort is being made to ease the situation. The Federal Republic, from its point of view, can only welcome these steps and it should not allow itself to be deterred by the constant propaganda accusations of the Soviets. Indeed our aim must be not to jeopardize our security and not to land ourselves in a situation in which we are deprived of American backing and are isolated. Furthermore, it must repeatedly be borne in mind that all these political measures can only receive our approval if they do not prevent the possibility of the reunification of our country in freedom.

It remains to be seen to what extent relations between the Soviet Union and Red China may also promote trends towards reduced tension. Hopes in this direction are not without foundation. Even today, the Soviet Union finds itself politically between two fires.

In the military field there are signs of similar considerations of relaxed tension. The idea of a reduction in troop strength which has already been mentioned, shall also contribute to a reduction in tension. As I have already said, however, it would be dangerous to undertake such a reduction without any similar action on the other side. The stationing of armed forces in the Federal Republic must be continued until the entire political situation undergoes some fundamental change. Advance action by reducing the strength of troops on the Western side alone, might dangerously upset the balance in Europe in favour of the East. Cuts in the conventional armed forces, moreover, would necessitate the premature use of nuclear force in order to be able to counteract inferiority in strength. This, however, could not be in the interests of the Federal Republic.

The idea of withdrawing tactical nuclear weapons from the Federal Republic has the same objective of reduced tension in view. The possibility of defending the Federal Republic would be decisively weakened so long as the nuclear shield over Europe cannot be replaced by seabound tactical nuclear forces–this might be possible later on.

This brings me to the decisive efforts to reduce tension in the nuclear field. Now that atomic experiments underground have been successfully banned – however, without the approval of

France and Red China – and an atomic clash in outer space has been excluded, the Treaty on the Non-Proliferation of Atomic Weapons is today in the forefront of our considerations. In principle this attempt (to prevent the spread of atomic weapons) is to be affirmed. The more countries that possess atomic weapons, the greater the danger of their being used. Even today there are already five powers that are in possession of such weapons, 14 others have atomic reactors which require some kind of control. But Red China and France have strongly rejected these efforts.

Nevertheless, one should persevere in this direction, although under two conditions: on the one hand the non-nuclear states should be protected against any political blackmail on the part of the nuclear powers and nuclear disarmament on the part of the great atomic powers should be sought. On the other hand, for all the non-nuclear powers, nuclear research and the peaceful use of atomic energy should be assured. This atomic energy will increasingly determine industrial and economic development in the world. Any state that has no share in it, would fall hopelessly behind and would be excluded from all major development.

The preliminary condition often mentioned in the past, namely that the possibility of common or joint nuclear solutions should not be prevented, should not be over-emphasized. This question will not arise until Europe has become united, and that will be a long process.

In rightly bringing up these two pre-conditions for discussion the Federal Republic should not force itself forward as a kind of battering ram for the non-nuclear powers. Other countries, and especially the neutrals like Sweden, India and Japan have the same interests.

One more thing. The fact that the Federal Republic is demanding a say in the planning of the actual use of nuclear weapons, remains irrevocable. No responsible government can unconditionally place the fate of its people in the hands of others, especially when its territory would be so affected by a nuclear strike as ours would be. It is especially in order to exercise a retarding function in such use of nuclear power, that this co-determination in planning is demanded. And it has been basically achieved by the new organization of a NATO Atomic Commitee.

What we do not want, however, is co-possession of nuclear forces. This cannot be stated often and clearly enough. The East is constantly arguing against us with assertions to the contrary. Even within the framework of reducing tension, this kind of propaganda must be constantly countered.

We see, therefore, how efforts to bring about a reduction of tension again and again bring up the question of security. It will only be possible to find a solution by means of a balancing of the two problems. But one should not despair in the face of this difficulty. The future of mankind may well depend on whether an acceptable synthesis between reduced tension and security is found.

In conclusion – Germany was, for centuries, the bridge between East and West. This historic function was always a difficult one. Today it is incomparably more difficult than in the past, on account of the division of our country and in view of the fact that East and West confront each other more harshly and directly than ever and because of the distrust that exists towards us not only in the East. However, if only on account of our geographical situation, our voice cannot be overheard when we are concerned with the task of putting new life into Europe and with bringing about peace in the world. Without the solution of the central European and thereby also of the German question, this aim will be unattainable.

What we must be concerned with is:

Firstly: no isolation – neither from America nor France. We have no choice between Paris or Washington. Both are of decisive importance to us. Washington primarily in the military sense and Paris politically.

Secondly: no appraisal of the Soviets on the basis of wishful thinking, but on realistic and dispassionate considerations, based on what the Soviets could do if they wanted to.

Thirdly: maintenance of the military presence in the Federal Republic to enable us to be equal to all political developments.

Fourthly: preservation of our economic and internal political stability as factors in our security.

And fifthly: Support for all efforts directed at reducing tension in so far as they do not endanger our security and in so far as they do not prevent the possibility of the reunification of our country.

Our policy is therefore faced by difficult and controversial problems. They can be solved not by stubbornly clinging to many of our former principles, but by adaptability and by new ideas. In this our policy must remain realistic and free from illusions, as Professor Jaspers once put it when he wrote, in effect:

Those who regard war as certain are helping to precipitate it by this view! Those who regard war as improbable, may well bring it about by their thoughtlessness! Only those who soberly weigh up all possibilities and prepare for all eventualities make the best contribution to its prevention.

And this should be the aim of us all.

Robert Pirk

"ORDERS IN CONTRADICTION"*

The answer to one of the great questions of our time, namely "how was it possible for the glorious German Army to be forced by a bloodthirsty dilettante to bleed to death in hopeless situations on innumerable battlefields?", is now given in a book written by a competent eye-witness who was directly involved. In its unequivocal clarity, this answer is indeed a moving one. Lieutenant-General Adolf Heusinger (retd.) whose name recently received prominence in the daily press on the occasion of his appointment as military adviser to the Federal Government in Bonn, served in the Operations Division of the Army High Command without a break from 1937 to July 20th 1944 – latterly as its chief. Immediately after the collapse of Germany in 1945, he drafted the plan for a chronicle of the war entitled "Befehl im Widerstreit" ("Orders in Contradiction") which was published a short time ago by Rainer Wunderlich-Verlag of Tübingen and Stuttgart. With understandable restraint, the title of this chronicle which, as regards contents and form is unique, is far too narrow and restricted and scarcely enables one to imagine the depth of psychological probe and the breadth of vision of a loyal and tradition-bound officer who, even in the most inhuman situations, remains a man of feeling.

Every line in this work which covers the period from the Treaty of Versailles to the ominous 8th of May 1945, is the convincing language of history. The author does not personally appear in the foreground, nor does he conceal himself. He simply

---

* *The following review of the book "Befehl im Widerstreit" by General (retd.) Heusinger is taken from the noted German language newspaper in the USA, "New Yorker Staatszeitung und Herold" of October 21st 1951. The book which was published by Rainer Wunderlich-Verlag, Tübingen, is also available in a French edition.*

takes his place as a soldier in the long chain of comrades of equal or higher rank (and also of jealous rivals), whom he lines up to submit their reports – to the "Führer" and, at the same time, to the international reading public that had previously been misled by war reports and post-war propaganda. He does not employ the explanatory and embellishing fantasy of the conventional writer, but relies almost exclusively on an admirable memory on which every feature of the "fateful hours of the German Army" since 1923, the year of the abortive putsch in Munich, is indelibly engraved. The tragic force of this epic of millions, that is played simultaneously on all continents, has a direct and impressive impact on the reader because it is not just a narrative or description but because it is shaped in the form of dialogues drawn from reality – a reality that far exceeds all fiction.

The names of the speakers are widely known and are not likely to be soon forgotten; they are Keitel, Göring, Jodl, Brauchitsch, Manstein, Paulus, Halder, Zeitzler, Stauffenberg, Stülpnagel, Heusinger. However, characteristic though each of their statements is and although the discussions ring true to the reader, based as they are on discreet secrecy between those of like mind and on crafty distrust between opponents, they all dramaturgically recede into the background to form that body of eagerly nodding and desperately shaking heads, wisely standing three paces away from the principal actor, Hitler. He is the one who always only wants to hear his own voice and who, at all times, treats them to his impressions and opinions unhindered. And they have striking effect; each of them means the senseless sacrificing of whole battalions.

When, at the end of 1939, Colonel-General von Brauchitsch, Supreme Commander of the Army made the warning remark that he still needed some time in order to overcome deficiencies in discipline, it is received with a fit of rage on the part of his chief: "I have used my whole party machine to supply the army with a young team which is better and more soldierly than anything we've had before. And you mean to say these young people do not meet the requirements? I'm sick of these objections. I bear the responsibility. I alone, not you or any other commander. I thank you."

No report on the situation at the Führer's Headquarters was without the obligatory "outbreak". The striking poverty of ideas is common to all. In monotonous repetition, the "Führer" demands faith (in him). Obedience, especially by the General Staff, the constant thorn in his side. – "When General Beck warns me against a conflict with Czechoslovakia and paints the terrors of a second world war on the wall, I will not stand for such instructions! The gentlemen should do what I demand of them and should be thankful that I assign them such tasks. I have no use for those who will not follow", – thus did he fume in the summer of 1938; and even in September 1944, after the Allied invasion and a whole chain of disastrous defeats, Lieutenant-General Heusinger hears him say: "I shall demand blind obedience of my generals just as I do of the little musketeer. I have already often regretted that I didn't purge my officer corps like Stalin did! But I *shall* do. They shall at last learn to obey without turning a hair."

The crusader against Bolshevism even cites Stalin as a model; he scoffs at himself and does not know how. The *leit-motiv* repeats itself. In 1942, when the Chief of the General Staff recommends "a certain degree of independence" for the Ukraine and the Baltic countries, he brusquely rejects the idea: "Don't you dare come to me with humanitarian methods in the East! They're all Asiatics. Stalin and the Tsar knew how they had to treat the people there."

At 12 noon on July 20th 1944 two dozen satellites assembled in the bunker at Rastenburg. Heusinger sits on the Führer's right. He is severely wounded when the bomb explodes which Stauffenberg had left behind in the brief-case. His illustrious neighbour suffers nothing but a tear in his trousers. The spectacular is followed by the satirical drama. Regardless of his bandages, Heusinger is taken away from hospital straight to the Gestapo cellars in Prinz-Albrecht-Straße where he is subjected to ceaseless cross-examination. But his superior intelligence upsets his tormentor's plan. The experience that one can even cope with the most evil of tyrants if one does not fear them, is once again convincingly proved.

The attempted assassination presents itself objectively and briefly noted, like a film sequence that is ready for shooting. The

Stalingrad episode impresses itself even more harshly and acutely on the reader. The Nemesis had to take its inevitable course because every attempt to eliminate its creator was doomed to failure from the outset. The battle-planner of Obersalzberg who cowardly evades the sight of the battlefields and is not interested in the only possible kind of mobile warfare, stubbornly clings to rigid struggle. He forbids evacuation. ("I shall not offer the world the spectacle that I was defeated at Stalingrad of all places!") Warned that this would mean sacrificing 200,000 men, he shrugged his shoulders and said: "Then I can't help it". After the debacle, the first best scapegoat, General Heim, is thrown into gaol. Göring, who never kept his frivolous promise to supply the city from the air, goes scot-free. – And yet, in spite of it all, the gambler was allowed to continue commanding unhindered, for more than two years, until 70 to 90 divisions had been sacrificed to his stubbornness. And yet the trained officers long since knew that the disaster was inevitable. "His authority grows from year to year", a major stated just after Munich; "even the worst doubters are gradually becoming silent as foreign countries repeatedly yield." A most up-to-date chapter that is strongly recommended to the men of the Pentagon for study; in addition they would learn something worth knowing about missed opportunities and groundless omissions which considerably contributed to a prolonging of the war and of the term of office of its instigator. To stop him from within was never possible – on account of the fatal double-track nature of the command machinery: OKW (Armed Forces High Command) and OKH (Army High Command) operating alongside each other, work basically against each other. When a capable general manages to assert himself at the Führer's Headquarters, he is immediately removed by the intrigues of Göring, Himmler and Goebbels. Yes-man Keitel nods his approval and the hard-headed dictator rapidly softens.

One Field Marshal after the other is dismissed. Resignations are strictly forbidden. "I am the one to decide how long you are to remain at your post." Heusinger also makes several attempts to secure his resignation, but without success. He foresees that many German officers' careers after the war will be ruined. Nevertheless his book is not an apologia and he rejects the new "stab-in-the-back" legend (" . . . it's the fault of those who did not believe in the Führer; he and the front were stabbed in the back"). This is a lame excuse if only because the majority of soldiers and the majority of Germans were much too gullible; they took their belief in the Führer so seriously that they failed to recognize his unworthiness and did not allow themselves to be deterred by disastrous failures and the most contemptuous contradictions.

The word "faith" occurs strikingly often in these dialogues. It rings of blasphemy when the Godless cynic himself abuses it – he who does not care a hoot for right and faith, who makes and rescinds laws as he pleases – laws whose guardians, because they let him escape, he sneeringly despises: "If the legal system had been in its place, I should never again have been allowed to return to political life after 1923."

Shattering revelations. But the conclusions drawn from them are encouraging to the reader. Heusinger frankly uncovers the conflict of conscience experienced by the generals, the gruelling dilemma between their oath of loyalty to the flag, and destiny, which "everyone had to fight out in his heart".

Here the author is on the track of the deeper problem. Those who bandy the phrase of collective guilt – which is just as non-existent as collective innocence – do not notice that their judgement is subject to the suggestive force of the age of the masses. Moral decisions are entirely a matter for the individual, a fact that many a German officer recognized too late. It is to be hoped that human insight to which, in this book, a military man has advanced, may blaze a trail.